A Coursebook for Oral English(4):
Public Speaking & Debate(Ⅱ)

英语口语教程(4)
——英语演讲与辩论(Ⅱ)

总主编 常俊跃
主　编 黄　滔
审　校 Marion Wyse
编　者 王　丹　陈　婧　张东黔　陆文玥

本套教材为以下项目的研究成果

☐ 国家哲学社会科学项目"英语专业基础阶段内容依托式教学改革研究"
☐ 辽宁省教育厅人文社会科学研究文科基地项目"对比修辞视野下的英语公共演讲教育研究"
☐ 辽宁省高等教育教学改革研究立项重点项目"语块驱动的对比修辞教学实践——英语公共演讲教学体系改革研究"
☐ 辽宁省教育厅优秀人才项目计划"内容依托式英语课程改革研究"

华中科技大学出版社
中国·武汉

图书在版编目(CIP)数据

英语口语教程(4)——英语演讲与辩论(Ⅱ)/黄滔主编. —武汉:华中科技大学出版社,2010.8(2021.6重印)
ISBN 978-7-5609-6174-3

Ⅰ.①英… Ⅱ.①黄… Ⅲ.①英语-演讲-语言艺术-高等学校-教材 ②英语-辩论-语言艺术-高等学校-教材 Ⅳ.①H319.9

中国版本图书馆 CIP 数据核字(2010)第 071545 号

英语口语教程(4)——英语演讲与辩论(Ⅱ)	黄 滔 主编

策划编辑:杨 鸥 刘 平
责任编辑:刘 平
封面设计:刘 卉
责任校对:李 琴
责任监印:朱 玢
出版发行:华中科技大学出版社(中国·武汉)   电话:(027)81321913
　　　　　武汉市东湖新技术开发区华工科技园   邮编:430223
录　　排:武汉佳年华科技有限公司
印　　刷:武汉开心印刷有限公司
开　　本:787mm×1092mm　1/16
印　　张:11.25
字　　数:278千字
版　　次:2021年6月第1版第8次印刷
定　　价:36.00元

本书若有印装质量问题,请向出版社营销中心调换
全国免费服务热线:400-6679-118　　竭诚为您服务
版权所有　侵权必究

总　序

随着我国英语教育的快速发展,英语专业长期贯彻的"以技能为导向"的课程建设理念及教学理念已经难以满足社会的需要。专家和教师们密切关注的现行英语专业教育大、中、小学英语教学脱节,语言、内容教学割裂,单纯语言技能训练过多,专业内容课程不足,学科内容课程系统性差,高、低年级内容课程安排失衡及其导致的学生知识面偏窄、知识结构欠缺、思辨能力偏弱、综合素质发展不充分等问题日益凸显。

针对上述问题,我们依托国家哲学社会科学项目"英语专业基础阶段内容依托式教学改革研究",以内容依托教学理论为指导理论,确定了如下改革思路。

（一）**更新语言教学理念,改革英语专业教学的课程结构**。在不改变专业总体培养目标和教学时限的前提下,对课程结构进行革命性的变革:改变传统单一的语言技能课程模式,实现内容课程与语言课程的融合,扩展学生的知识面,提高学生的语言技能。

（二）**开发课程自身潜力,同步提高专业知识和语言技能**。内容依托课程本身也同时关注内容和语言,把内容教学和语言教学有机结合。以英语为媒介,系统教授专业内容;以专业内容为依托,在使用语言过程中提高语言技能,扩展学生的知识面。

（三）**改革教学方法手段,全面提高语言技能和综合素质**。依靠内容依托教学在方法上的灵活性,通过问题驱动、输出驱动等方法调动学生主动学习,把启发式、任务式、讨论式、结对子、小组活动、课堂发表等行之有效的活动与学科内容教学有机结合,提高学生的语言技能,激发学生的兴趣,培养学生的自主性和创造性,提升思辨能力和综合素质。

本项改革突破了我国英语专业英语教学大纲规定的课程结构,改变了英语专业基础阶段通过开设单纯的听、说、读、写四种语言技能课提高学生语言技能的传统课程建设理念,对英语课程及教学方法进行了创新性的改革。首创了英语专业基础阶段具有我国特色的内容、语言融合的课程体系;率先开发了适合英语专业基础阶段的内容依托课程;系统开发了英语国家历史、地理、社会文化、欧洲文化、中国文化、跨文化交际、《圣经》与文化、功能英语交际、情景英语交际、英语演讲与辩论等教材,以崭新的途径实现英语专业教育的总体培养目标。

经过七年的酝酿、准备、实验,教学改革取得了鼓舞人心的结果。

（一）**构建了英语专业基础阶段内容依托课程与语言课程融合的课程体系**。新的课程体系改变了传统单一的听、说、读、写语言技能课程模式,实现了内容依托课程和语言技能课程两种模块的融合;课程包含综合英语、听力、语音、写作、功能英语交际、情景英语交际、英语演讲与辩论、英国历史文化、英国自然人文地理、英国社会文化、美国历史文化、美国自然人文地理、美国社会文化、澳新加社会文化、欧洲文化、中国文化、跨文化交际、《圣经》与文化;语言技能课程密切关注英语语言技能的发展,内容依托课程不仅关注系统的学科内容,而且也关注综合语言技能的培养。在课程外和课程内两个层面把内容教学和语言教学有机结合,通过内容教学培养学生综合语言运用能力,扩展学生的知识面,提高学生的综合素质和多元文化意识,从根本上改变英语专业学生知识面偏窄、综合素质偏低的问题。

（二）系统开发了相关国家的史、地、社会文化以及跨文化交际课程资源。在内容依托教学理论的指导下，在实施内容依托教学的关键期——英语专业的第一学年，成功开设了英国和美国的历史、地理、社会文化等课程。第二学年开设澳、新、加等国社会文化，欧洲文化，中国文化，跨文化交际，《圣经》与文化等课程。内容依托教材改变了传统的组织模式，系统组织了教学内容，设计了新颖的栏目板块，设计的活动也丰富多样，教学实践中受到了学生的广泛欢迎。此外还开发了开设课程所需要的大量资源。

（三）牵动了教学手段和教学方法的改革，取得了突出的教学效果。在内容依托教学理论的指导下，教师的教学理念、教学方法、教学手段得到更新。通过问题驱动、输出驱动等活动调动学生主动学习，把启发式、任务式、讨论式、结对子、小组活动、课堂展示、多媒体手段等行之有效的活动与学科内容教学有机结合，激发学生的兴趣，培养学生的自主性和创造性，提高学生的语言技能，提升思辨能力和综合素质。曾有专家和教师担心新的课程体系会对语言技能发展产生消极影响。实验数据证明，改革不仅没有对学生的语言技能发展和语言知识的学习产生消极影响，而且还产生了多方面的积极影响。此外，对学生学科知识学习产生的巨大积极影响更是传统课程体系不可能做到的。

（四）提高了教师的科研意识和科研水平，取得了丰硕的教研成果。项目开展以来，团队对内容依托教学问题进行了系列研究，活跃了整个教学单位的科研气氛，科研意识和科研水平也得到很大提高。课题组已经撰写研究论文25篇，在国际、国内学术研讨会交流12篇，在国际学术期刊World Englishes、国内外语类核心期刊《外语与外语教学》、《中国外语》、《外语教学理论与实践》等发表研究论文8篇。

教学改革开展以来，每次成果发布都引起强烈反响。在2008年3月的第三届中国外语教学法国际研讨会上，与会的知名外语教育专家戴炜栋教授等对这项改革给予关注，博士生导师蔡基刚教授认为本项研究"具有导向性作用"。在2008年5月的"第二届全国英语专业院系主任高级论坛"上，研究成果得到知名专家、博士生导师王守仁教授和与会其他专家及教授的积极评价。在2008年7月的中国英语教学研究会东北地区年会上，改革的系列成果引起与会专家的强烈反响，研究论文获得3个优秀论文一等奖，3个二等奖，1个三等奖。2008年11月，在中国英语教学研究会年会上，成果再次引起与会专家的强烈反响，博士生导师石坚教授等给予了高度评价。2008年10月和12月，本项改革成果分别获得大连外国语学院教学研究成果一等奖和辽宁省优秀教学成果一等奖。2009年获得第六届国家优秀教学成果二等奖。在2009年5月的"第三届全国英语专业院系主任高级论坛"上，本项改革成果再次赢得专家和同行的赞誉。在2009年10月的中国英语教学研究会2009年会上，本项改革成果在主旨发言中向我国英语界同仁发布，得到了戴炜栋、文秋芳等知名专家、同行的高度肯定。

目前，该项成果已经在全国英语专业教育领域引起广泛关注。它触及了英语专业的教学大纲，影响了课程建设的理念，引领了英语专业的教学改革，改善了教学实践，必将对未来英语专业教育的发展产生积极影响。

本项改革开展过程中得到了全国各地专家的关注、支持、帮助和肯定。衷心感谢戴炜栋教授、王守仁教授、文秋芳教授、石坚教授、蔡基刚教授、杨忠教授等前辈给予的鼓励和支持，衷心感谢大连外国语学院校领导孙玉华教授、赵忠德教授、杨俊峰教授及其他各位领导的大力支持，感谢大连外国语学院教务处刘宏处长、姜凤春副处长以及工作人员们在改革实验中给予的大力支持，感谢大连外国语学院科研处张雪处长和工作人员们给予的热情帮助，感谢大连外国语学院英语学院领导的全力支持和同事们的无私帮助以及团队成员的共同努力。同时也真诚感谢为我们内容依托教学改革提供丰富教学材料的国内外专家。特别感谢华中科技大学出版社的杨鸥编辑和刘平编辑，没有他们对新教学理念的认同，没有他们对英语专业教育的关注和支持，这套教材不可能如此迅速地面世。

  作为一项探索，我们团队成员虽然为打造这套精品教材做出了巨大努力，但由于水平所限，教材中难免存在疏漏和不足，希望全国各地的同仁不吝赐教，希望使用本套教材的师生提出改进意见和建议，以期不断完善教材，为提高英语专业教育的质量共同努力。

常俊跃

2010 年 6 月

于大连外国语学院

前　言

社会的发展总是在对人的能力提出新的要求和挑战。21世纪被称为"表达的年代"（an age of expression），这意味着人的沟通能力已经被提高到了一个非常关键的地位。演讲作为一种强有力的表达手段和沟通手段，日益受到越来越多的领导者、教育者和学习者的重视。

同时，在多样、复杂的国际环境中，跨文化的对话和话语对抗日益频繁，涉及商务、政治、科研、教育等各个行业和领域。英语是国际交流中必不可少的语言工具，需要用英语进行演讲的情形包括论文宣读、商业展示、专题报告、声明、谈判、抗辩等等。因此，在跨文化的沟通活动中，用英语演讲的能力显得尤其重要和便利。良好的英语演讲能力能帮助演讲者实现强大的影响力、说服力和感染力，从而在跨文化的语言对抗中立于不败之地。

英语演讲能力是英语综合知识和英语综合能力的全面体现，同时也是演讲者思维能力、表达能力和人格魅力的集中体现。中国学生学习用英语演讲不是一件简单的事，这是因为除了综合知识之外，英语的修辞取向和汉语的修辞取向有明显的区别，所以学习英语演讲和辩论需要在掌握相关知识的同时攻克语言和技巧（即修辞）这两个难关。

本教材在设计中多管齐下，旨在帮助中国的英语学习者解决语言和修辞难题。教材在传授演讲和辩论知识的基础上，注重实际的语言操练，这使得本套教材不同于普通的英语演讲教材，具备很强的实用性和可操作性。

本教材主要有以下几个方面的优势和特点：

1. **注重修辞理念**：演讲是修辞最直接、最精华的体现和成果。然而，中外对比修辞研究的最新成果表明，中国学生在演讲稿中所表现出的修辞取向与英语的修辞取向存在较大差异，尤其体现在语篇模式建构上。因此，本套教材在 Knowledge Input 部分着重帮助学习者理解英、汉语篇修辞的差异，引导学习者遵循英语演讲的修辞模式进行语篇建构和观点陈述，从而提升演讲的修辞价值，提升其说服力和感染力。

2. **强调语言输入**：本教材中的 Lexical Power Build-Up 部分为学习者提供了大量实用性很强的预置语块，适用于各种类型的演讲场合和演讲目的。这些语块的选择是以英语演讲修辞理念为基础的，所以对语块的操练和运用不仅能提升学习者的语言能力，而且能进一步深化对修辞思想的理解，使学习者的演讲风格更加趋近英语演讲修辞的要求。

3. **练习多种多样**：本教材在 Comprehensive Practice 中为教师和学习者设计了不同层次、不同目的、不同形式的练习。练习主要以口语形式完成，包括即时理解能力训练、批判性思维训练、语言运用能力训练、演讲和辩论训练、团队合作训练等。这些练习目的明确，具有很强的操作性和娱乐性，教师和学习者可以根据实际情况选择使用，实现在经历中学习，获得最佳的学习效果。

4. **优质素材输入**：本教材中选用的演讲范例和名篇兼顾各种类型、各种风格，具有很强的时效性和针对性，从质量和数量上均能满足各种学习层次的学习者的需求。

5. **内容轻松活泼**：为了补充多样性的学习内容并深化对修辞思想的理解，教材在

Amusement Park 栏目加入了电影中的演讲片段欣赏和歌词欣赏。这些寓教于乐的教材内容不仅为学习者课后的学习提供了素材,而且丰富了语言输入的形式,有助于提升学习者的学习兴趣。

6. 涵盖比赛训练: 现在国内各种英语演讲、辩论比赛日益频繁,因此本教材加入了部分比赛项目的训练内容,包括说服性有备演讲、即兴演讲、回答提问、议会制辩论等各项重要比赛内容。

7. 兼顾阶段需求: 英语专业四级口语考试是英语专业二年级学生面临的重大考试,本教材充分考虑了学生阶段性的需要,根据专业四级口试的要求设立了 New Hurdles 板块,提供了系统的训练材料,组织了系统的训练,以帮助学生在口语测试中充分展示自己的表达能力。

为打造这套精品教材,我们全体编写人员做出了巨大努力。此外,陈胜国、刘男、刘立红、马明洁、解放、许敬、郑兴华等也参与了本书的校对工作。我们希望我们的努力能为推动英语专业教学改革、探索英语专业人才培养的新路做出有益的贡献。

编　者

2010 年 6 月

于大连外国语学院英语学院

Contents

Part Three Polishing Speaking Skills

Unit 17	Narrative Speech with Examples	(3)
Unit 18	Audience-Centred Speeches	(13)
Unit 19	Speech Topics and Plans	(23)
Unit 20	Logos — Rational Appeal	(33)
Unit 21	Pathos — Emotional Appeal	(44)
Unit 22	Ethos — Credibility Appeal	(54)
Unit 23	Persuasive Speeches on Questions of Value	(64)
Unit 24	Rhetoric for Public Policy Speeches	(75)

Part Four English Speaking Contest

Unit 25	Prepared Speech in English Speaking Contests	(87)
Unit 26	Impromptu Speech in English Speaking Contests	(97)
Unit 27	Q & A in English Speaking Contests	(106)

Part Five Debating Skills

Unit 28	Basics of Debate	(117)
Unit 29	Evidence for Debate	(127)
Unit 30	Logic in Debate	(136)
Unit 31	Questioning and Team Skills in Debate	(145)
Unit 32	Parliamentary Debate	(155)
参考文献		(169)

Part Three
Polishing Speaking Skills

Unit 17

Narrative Speech with Examples

> The basic rule of human nature is that powerful people speak slowly and subservient people quickly — because if they do not speak fast nobody will listen to them.
>
> —Michael Caine[1]

Unit Goals

- To learn to use information, explanation, examples, facts, or illustrations to put ideas across
- To learn to use transitions to increase coherence
- To learn how to organize examples and details
- To learn to manipulate your tempo when you speak

Warm-Up

1. For what purposes do people need to use examples? Or in what ways do you think examples can be helpful?
2. Can you give examples to tell how many different ways you could use a piece of brick?

Knowledge Input

Organization of Examples and Details

When we need to give examples and details in our speech, it is necessary to consider the order of their presentation. Unlike narrative, where sentences are ordered chronologically, and descriptions, where sentences are logically organized on a spatial principle, the sentences in the expository paragraph follow no prescribed or set pattern of organization. The ordering depends on the subject and often on the speaker's logic. There are, however, some common patterns that might be considered guidelines.

Order of importance — saving the best for last: Often, when you are developing a topic sentence with examples and details, one of the examples is more impressive than the others. Since audiences generally remember what they hear last, and since it is a good idea to leave a good impression on the audience, it is wise to place the most impressive example at the end of the paragraph. Study the following part of a speech, and note that the last example is the most startling one.

A search through etymologies will reveal some examples of words which have narrowed in meaning since their early days. **Barbarian** *was originally a vague designation for a foreigner of any kind;* **garage**, *when it was borrowed from France, meant "a place for storage." In the United States,* **lumber** *has specialized to mean "timber or sawed logs especially prepared for use," but in Britain the word still retains its more generally meaning of "unused articles". ... Perhaps the most startling specialization has taken place with the word* **girl**; *even as late as Chaucer's time, it was used to mean "a young person of either sex"!*

Order of familiarity — from the more familiar to the less familiar: When the details in the expository paragraph are mostly factual, it is common to begin with the most obvious or familiar detail and move toward the less obvious or less familiar detail. This is the pattern of the following paragraph about the expense of smoking cigarettes. The writer begins with details that most people would consider when thinking about expense: the price. Then the writer discusses the less obvious or familiar expense of smoking cigarettes: the cleaning. Read the paragraph and note how the writer connects the more obvious expense to the less obvious expense.

Smoking cigarettes can be an expensive habit. Considering that the average price per pack of cigarettes is about $2.50, people who smoke two packs of cigarettes a day spend $5 per day on their habit. But the cost of cigarettes is not the only expense cigarette smokers incur. Since cigarette smoke has an offensive odor that permeates clothing, stuffed furniture and carpeting, smokers often find that they must have these items cleaned more frequently than nonsmokers do. This hidden expense does contribute to making cigarette smoking an expensive habit.

Order of time — from the past to the present: When the details and examples in a paragraph are taken from history or are events that have taken place in the past, it is often a good idea to order the examples according to chronology.

The seventeenth century was a period of great advances in science. For example, early in this century, Galileo perfected the telescope and in 1609 published "The Sidereal Messenger". Only a few years later, the Dutch scientist Anton van Leeuwenhoek performed pioneering research with the microscope, discovering that fleas and other minute creatures come from eggs rather than being spontaneously generated. Not long after this, William Harvey, an English physician, discovered the method by which blood circulates in humans. Finally, in the 1660s, Isaac Newton discovered the law of gravitation and the laws governing the physics of light, and he also invented differential calculus.

Knowledge Internalization

1. Pair Work

Talk with your partner about the order you usually follow. Give some examples of the occasions when you can use the different orders mentioned above.

2. Group Work

Study the following topic sentence and its supporting details and discuss them with your group members. Rearrange the support so that each detail is in its most logical position. Remember, there is no set order, but you must be able to justify your choices.

Topic sentence: China has suffered from some of the worst disasters in history.

a. The worst disaster of all time occurred in 1931, when the Yellow River flooded, killing 3.7 million people.

b. On January 24, 1556, 830 000 people died in an earthquake.

c. In 1642, 300 000 Chinese perished as a result of flood waters.

d. In 1887, the Yellow River flooded, causing the death of 900 000 Chinese.

e. The Year 1927 saw another devastating earthquake, killing 200 000 people.

f. There was an earthquake in Tangshan in 1976 that killed 242 000 people.

g. In 1982 and 1983, over 1 700 people died from floods.

h. In 2008, over 80 000 people lost their lives in the Wenchuan earthquake in Sichuan Province.

Lexical Power Build-Up

1. Lexical Input

Here are some useful language chunks for citing examples. Practice them until you can say them automatically, but pay special attention to their pronunciation and intonation.

For example, / For instance, / To be specific, salmon are kept in ponds.

In this example, / In this case, / In this instance, fish are transferred to rivers.

A river is an example / an instance / an illustration of a habitat.

Fish like / such as salmon are cultivated.

By way of illustration, Smith shows how the data for...

A classic / well-known example of this is...

X is a good example / illustration of...
X illustrates this point / shows this point clearly.
This can be illustrated briefly by...
Another example /An additional example is...

2. Lexical Input

Here are some useful language chunks for transitions which glue your examples together. Practice them until you can say them automatically, but pay special attention to their pronunciation and intonation.

Perhaps the most startling/tragic example is...
Let's begin with the familiar example of...
An additional example for this is...
Moreover, / Besides,...
Afterwards / Later,...
Last but not least,...
Finally,...
A more recent /typical example is...
If this incident is not enough to show the severity of the situation, let's look at another more shocking example.

3. Pair Work

Work with your partner and try to add more expressions to the list above.

4. Pair Work

Make a generalization about a person you know, and then give supporting examples. For instance, you might begin with, "My little brother has done some amusing things." You could support this generalization with several examples of amusing things he had done. Try to use a proper order to organize the examples. Follow the "generalization — example — transition — example — transition — example — conclusion pattern".

Then tell your partner about them.

Comprehensive Input

Sample One

Below is a short part of speech about superstition in the United States. Pay attention to the transitions used between different examples.

Superstition in the United States

Although the United States has become an advanced technological country, many old-fashioned superstitions still remain. For instance, when walking down a street in New

York City past ingeniously² built skyscrapers, you might see a sophisticated New Yorker walk around instead of under a ladder. Of course, he or she knows that walking under a ladder brings bad luck. Or, should a black cat wander from a back alley to that same bustling street, some people would undoubtedly cross to the other side of the street to avoid letting a black cat cross their path. Moreover, it is true that most buildings in the United States do not have a thirteenth floor and many theaters do not have a thirteenth row. Again, we all know that 13 is an unlucky number. Besides, if you take a drive through Pennsylvania Dutch country, you will see large colorful symbols called hex signs³ attached to houses and barns. Of course, the people who live there say they are just for decoration, but sometimes I wonder.

Sample Two

Surnames

When surnames began appearing in Europe 800 years ago, a person's identity and occupation were often intertwined³. A surname was a direct link between who a person was and what that person did. For example, Taylor is the Old English spelling of tailor, and Clark is derived from clerk, an occupation of considerable status during the Middle Ages because it required literacy. Also, the names Walker, Wright, Carter, Stewart, and Turner indicate occupations. A walker was someone who cleaned cloth; a wright was a carpenter or metalworker; a carter was someone who drove a cart; a steward was a person in charge of a farm or estate; and a turner worked a lathe. One of the few occupational surnames reflecting the work of women is Webster, which refers to a female weaver.

Comprehensive Practice

1. Pair Work

How many examples are given in the above speeches? Underline the transitions between different examples, and discuss whether you can find other words or expressions to fit in the transitional parts.

2. Solo Work

Plan a speech about superstitions in China. Give specific examples to illustrate your idea. Remember to use transitions between your examples. Get ready to talk in front of your classmates.

3. Solo Work

Tempo

The rate at which you produce sounds is called tempo. When we speak, we should moderately vary our tempo, because doing either to the extreme can turn off our audience. Our tempo is also affected by pauses. Sometimes a brief moment of silence can convey much to an audience. So do not be afraid to use pauses when appropriate. It is also better to pause a moment than to fill the air with "ums," "uhs," and "you knows," which are really vocalized pauses.

Practice the speech you've just planned about superstitions in China. Learn to control your tempo. Do not speak too quickly or too slowly.

4. Group Work

Now give the speech about superstitions in China in your group. Give each other suggestions to improve. Choose the best speaker in your group to speak in front of the class.

5. Solo Work

Pollution is one of the top concerns all over the world. Plan a short speech about how serious the pollution problem has become. You need to use specific examples to support your idea. Then practice giving the speech. Make recordings of your own voice and try to find your own strengths and weaknesses.

6. Group Work

Every culture has proverbs. Some popular ones in English are "The early bird catches the worm" and "A stitch in time saves nine." Think of a popular proverb in Chinese and translate it into good English. Form groups of four. Each group is to choose their own proverb, and all the group members should tell anecdotes from their lives that show the truth of this statement.

Extra Input

The following excerpt is from Stéphane Dion's Response to PM Stephen Harper on Opposition Coalition, delivered on 3rd, December 2008, in Parliament Hill, Ottawa, Ontario.

Pay attention to the specific examples he uses. Would the speech have the same effect if he omitted the examples? What effect do the examples create?

My dear fellow Canadians,

Canada is facing the impacts of the global economic crisis. Our economy is on the verge of a recession. Canadians are worried about losing their jobs, their homes, and their savings. Every economist in the country is predicting increased job losses and deficits for the next few years. The federal government has a duty to act and help Canadians weather this storm...We will gather with leaders of industry and labor to work in a collaborative but urgent manner to protect jobs. To stimulate the economy and create good well-paid jobs we will not only accelerate already planned investments, but invest significantly more in our country's infrastructure. We will help our cities like Vancouver, Calgary, Toronto, Montreal or Halifax build modern, efficient public transit systems. And we will invest in our rural communities so that cherished ways of life are protected for future generations. We can stimulate our economy through investments in clean energy, water and our gateways. We will invest in our manufacturing, forestry and automotive sectors to protect and create jobs. We believe that in these tough economic times the government has a role to play to ensure that those who are doing their share for the prosperity of our country can continue to provide for the well-being of their families...

New Hurdles

1. Retelling

Listen to the passage and retell it immediately after you have heard it.

The Giving Tree

A long time ago, there was a huge apple tree. A little boy loved to come and play around it everyday. He climbed to the tree top, ate the apples, took a nap under the shadow. He loved the tree and the tree loved to play with him.

Time went by. The little boy had grown up and he no longer played around the tree everyday. One day, the boy came back to the tree and he looked sad.

"Come and play with me," the tree asked the boy.

"I am no longer a kid. I do not play around trees anymore." The boy replied, "I want toys. I need money to buy them."

"Sorry, but I do not have money. But you can pick all my apples and sell them. So, you will have money." The boy was very excited.

He grabbed all the apples on the tree and left happily.

The boy never came back after he picked the apples. The tree was sad.

One day, the boy returned and the tree was so excited. "Come and play with me." The tree said.

"I do not have time to play. I have to work for my family. We need a house. Can you help me?"

"Sorry, but I do not have a house. But you can chop off my branches to build your house."

So the boy cut all the branches of the tree and left happily. The tree was glad to see him happy but the boy never came back since then. The tree was again lonely and sad.

One hot summer day, the boy returned and the tree was delighted. "Come and play with me!" The tree said.

The boy said, "I am sad and getting old. I want to go sailing to relax myself. Can you give me a boat?"

"Use my trunk to build your boat. You can sail far away and be happy."

So the boy cut the tree trunk to make a boat. He went sailing and did not showed up for a long time.

Finally, the boy returned after many years. "Sorry, my boy. But I do not have anything for you anymore. No more apples for you." The tree said.

"I do not have teeth to bite." The boy replied.

"No more trunk for you to climb on."

"I am too old for that now." The boy said.

"I really can not give you anything. The only thing left is my dying roots." The tree said with tears.

"I do not need much now, just a place to rest. I am tired after all these years." The boy replied.

"Good! Old tree roots are the best place to lean on and rest. Come, come sit down with me and rest."

The boy sat down and the tree was glad and smiled through its tears.

This is a story of everyone. The tree is our parent. When we were young, we loved to play with Mom and Dad. When we are grown up, we leave them, only to come to them when we need something or when we are in trouble. No matter what, parents will always be there and give everything they could to make us happy. You may think the boy is cruel to the tree, but that's how all of us are treating our parents.

2. Talking on a Given Topic

Recollect an unforgettable experience of making money. You have three minutes to prepare your talk and then tell it to your partner.

3. Role Play

The task involves two students, Student A and Student B. Each has a specified role as follows. Although the situation is the same, your roles are different. Learn about the role you want to play. Your preparation time is three minutes. Your conversation is limited to four minutes. Student A and Student B are talking about whether going to college is the best way to fulfill one's dreams.

Student A: You believe going to college is definitely the best way and the only way to fulfill one's dreams. You should give examples to support your idea. Remember you should start the conversation.

Student B: You do not agree with A and believe going to college is sometimes unnecessary for some people. Fulfilling one's dream has nothing to do with a college degree. You should also give examples to support your idea.

Notes

1. Michael Caine(1933 —): British-born American actor, acting teacher.
2. ingeniously: skillfully; wittily; cleverly
3. intertwine: to join or become joined by twining together.

Amusement Park

1. Movie to Enjoy

See the following movie and share your personal view with your classmates next week.

The Shawshank Redemption (1994)

The film portrays Andy spending nearly two decades in Shawshank State Prison, a fictional penitentiary in Maine, and his friendship with Red, a fellow inmate. The movie received favorable reviews from critics and has since enjoyed a remarkable life on cable television, home video, and DVD. It continues to be hailed by critics and audiences alike, 16 years after its initial release, and is ranked among the greatest films of all time.

Special Highlight

A speech scene in *The Shawshank Redemption* is when the warden of the prison gives the "Welcome to prison" speech to the new arrivals. In the speech, the warden advises the prisoners to study the Bible and follow instructions.

Do you feel the ironic effect of the speech, or the ironic effect of the whole movie? What might be the meaning of the Bible in this movie?

2. Song to Enjoy

Complete the lyrics while you are enjoying the song "Tell Me Why" by Declan Galbraith.

What is the song about? When the singer sings "tell me why", what answer is he asking for? What is he against and what is he for?

In my dreams, children sing
A song of love for every boy and girl
The sky is blue, the fields are green
And laughter is the language of the world
Then I wake and all I see is a world full of people in need
...

Every day, I ask myself
what will I have to do to be a man
Do I have to stand and fight
To prove to everybody who I am
Is that what my life is for?
To waste in a world full of war
...

Tell me why, (why) does it have to be like this
Tell me why, (why) is there something I have missed
Tell me why, (why) cause I do not understand
When so many need somebody
We do not give a helping hand
Tell me why (why why, does the tigers run?)
...

3. Community Learning

Many people say that great artists are unique. Do you agree? What makes artists unique? Give examples to support the idea. Choose one student to give a speech about it and the other students give suggestions and comments on his/her performance.

Unit 18

Audience-Centred Speeches

> Make sure you have finished speaking before your audience has finished listening.
> — Dorothy Sarnoff[1]

Unit Goals

- To learn to analyze the audience before writing and speaking
- To learn to empathize with the audience when speaking
- To learn to regulate the audience when speaking
- To be able to apply the audience-centered approach to your speech

Warm-Up

1. Recall your public speaking experience. Who did you consider to be the most frightening, or most supportive audience? What were they like?
2. Are you more comfortable with a familiar audience or are you better off when the audience are total strangers? Why?
3. Have you noticed any difference between Chinese audiences and western audiences? What are the differences? Can you find any reasons for such differences?

Knowledge Input

Taking an Audience-Centered Approach

Have you ever considered, before asking someone for help, who they are, how they can help you, or whether they are capable of doing so? It is also true with a persuasive speech, which will be made successful only when the speaker can better serve the audience. The degree to which your audience will be convinced or persuaded largely depends on how well you connect with your audience.

To reach out successfully to your listeners requires knowing who they are and what they need, understanding their mind, and meeting their needs. An audience-centered approach could help to tailor your persuasive speech to fit the audience. It includes considering the audience's experience, interest level, motivation, cultural background, familiarity with your topic, etc. An adequate audience survey prior to the event of the speech will enable you to be better oriented in the choice of your purpose, strategies and language. In analyzing your audience, you can follow the simple steps below:

Step 1: Identify the needs of the audience. You should approach the situation from the audience's point of view and make clear what their objective is for coming to your speech. Why is the audience here? What do they expect from your speech? What sort of material are they looking for? Are they seeking information, inspiration or entertainment? These factors have to be considered when planning your speech.

Step 2: Assess the audience's interest, knowledge and attitude. You should tailor your message to the audience's disposition toward the topic. Be sure you can answer the following questions concerning the audience: What is the knowledge level of the audience? Are they well informed of the subject matter? Is the audience eager to listen? Or will they be hostile to your message? The interest and attitude of your listeners can be extremely important in determining how you handle the material.

Step 3: Decide on your message, persuasion strategy and language according to what you know about the audience. You need to narrow the topic down to one central theme or message, but you should do this from the audience's perspective, rather than your own. Plan your strategy in a way so that your message will be easily accepted and well-received by the audience. For example, when you take your audience's skepticism into account, you may have to make special efforts to establish the scientific credibility of your speech. Then you have much better opportunity to make your arguments more convincing to the audience. Finally, the language you use should suit the audience's knowledge level and be able to stimulate more interest in the topic.

Step 4: Establish a rapport with the audience and track down how they are listening. An audience-centered approach towards public speaking also requires effective delivery skills.

You should connect with your audience, appearing natural. Do not breeze through your speech. Instead, pause for a while or slow down a bit, especially at those points you want to emphasize. You should also establish eye contact with your listeners and observe how they are listening. You may need to adjust your speed, volume, or strategy when you see signs of negative feedback from the audience.

As a public speaker, it is an art to cultivate listening, and make your speech something the audience will not only hear, but something they will want to hear. In trying to do so, understanding the audience and speaking from the audience's point of view are crucial.

Knowledge Internalization

1. Pair Work

Recall your experience of giving or listening to a speech. Discuss with your partner how the audience's interest, knowledge, attitude, etc. may change with different subject matter and different physical settings. Reinforce your understanding of the importance of the audience-centered approach.

2. Pair Work

1) Tell your partner your most often used "opening gambit" to make a good impression on your audience.
2) Does your "opening gambit" always work? Tell a success story and a failure story if you have any.
3) Discuss with your partner how you can improve your "opening gambit" with the audience-centered approach.

3. Group Work

Discuss the following questions in groups of four or five and then report the result of your discussion to the class.

1) When you are faced with a skeptical audience, what strategies may help you win their favor?
2) When you are faced with a somewhat hostile audience, what strategies may help you break the ice?
3) When you are faced with a very friendly and supportive audience, what strategies may help you achieve your purpose?
4) What other types of audience can you expect? What strategies may suit these types best?

Lexical Power Build-Up

1. Lexical Input

One of Chinese students' common problems is the overuse of "I", "I think", or "I believe" regardless of the situation or the purpose of the speech. This may be indicative of the tendency among Chinese students to be more subjective and self-centered than is considered appropriate or welcome. This habit may be rooted in Chinese culture, for in the history of Chinese rhetoric, there has been an emphasis on the dominant position of the speaker rather than of the audience.

In order to convey a more audience-centered "you-attitude" when giving a speech, you can learn to:

1) *Vary the subject.*
Omit "I think" and begin your sentence with the subject in object clause.

2) *Use other "time-fillers" when hesitating.*
Expressions such as *well, basically, as a matter of fact, as far as... is concerned, let's see*, etc. would function more naturally than "I think" when you are trying to buy some time to think.

3) *Use other expressions to replace "I think".*
When expressing an opinion, you do not have to always begin with "I think". Instead, you can begin with:

It would be reasonable to say...
The idea that... is...
It can not be denied that...
There is a point in saying...
The truth is...
The point is...
Believe it or not,... etc.

2. Pair Work

Reconstruct the following sentences, omitting the unnecessary use of "I think", "I believe", etc., using the examples listed above.

1) In my opinion, global warming is not a warning, but it is already a reality.
2) I firmly believe that every country, regardless of its development stage, should take responsibility for emission control.
3) I believe developed countries are the bigger emitters, so they should take major responsibility for cutting emission.
4) I do not think the love of one's country lies in words or sentiments, but in actions.
5) I think the best way to start energy conservation is recycling.

6) My opinion is that language learning depends more on input than on output.

3. Group Work

Work in a group of four or five and brainstorm to find more expressions for hesitation and expressing opinions. Report your group's results to the class for everyone to share.

Comprehensive Input

Below is the excerpt of a sample speech on the topic of "gender selection".

For centuries, couples have tried to choose the genders of their children. One recent study has shown that more than forty percent of couples worldwide would choose the sex of their child if possible. Is the ability to select a child's gender really a good thing, though?

Supporters of gender selection have a strong argument and quite a bit of support from a number of different places. Dr. Ronald Ericsson, called Dr. Sperm by many, has been marketing a home test kit to help couples choose the gender of their child. As a result, he's quite familiar with both sides of the issue. Dr. Ericsson believes it is a human rights issue. He suggests that because the technology is available, people should be allowed to use it.

Strange, that after all the destructive things we've done with technology, someone would say that because it is available we should use it. Just because we can, doesn't mean we should.

The thing most supporters of gender selection do not know is that the gender selection process is still in the beginning stages of development, so scientists do not get it right 100% of the time. As a result, couples can spend thousands of dollars trying to create a baby of their choice, only to be disappointed in the end.

Not only is gender selection risky, but it can create sex distortion ratios, particularly in countries where one sex is the preferred member of society.

Supporters of gender selection, though, have come up with an answer to this one as well. Dr. Suresh Nayak suggested that the fear that sex selection would change the natural ratios was unfounded because the practice is only used by a fraction of couples who can afford it. That fact, though, may soon change.

As the procedures get increasingly cheaper, more couples are taking advantage of them. Fertility clinics are literally swamped with couples trying to create a designer baby. By the end of 2004, more than 4000 cases of successful gender selected babies were reported. Many clinics are starting to study the procedure to make it more available to couples.

Huston's Baylor College of Medicine started a study of 200 couples in 2005 to examine the gender selection process. This procedure will, quite clearly, distort the natural gender ratios if enough people can afford the procedure, and if doctors and scientists have their way, everyone will soon be able to afford it.

...

Comprehensive Practice

1. Solo Work

Read the speech aloud to your classmates. Pay attention to the response of your audience as you are reading to them. Adjust your speed, volume and tempo when necessary.

2. Pair Work

Discuss the following questions with your partner.
1) What attitude do you expect the audience to have towards this topic?
2) What strategy does the speaker follow to expose the wrongness of sex selection? Do you find this strategy effective?
3) If you were a supporter of gender selection, how would this speech affect you?
4) How does the speaker make the speech sound credible? What do you think is the effect of credibility on the audience?

3. Solo Work

Observe how the speaker manages to remain objective and rational by avoiding using too many first-person sentences. Learn this technique and use it in your own speech.

4. Class Work

Your class choose to go to watch a football game or a fashion show — but not both — for Students' Night. As the organizer of the event, you deliver a speech to persuade your classmates to go with you to the game/show. Take your classmates' different interests and attitudes into consideration.

Then the class should comment on the speaker's effectiveness in his/her persuasion.

5. Solo Work

Prepare different versions of a two-minute presentation on the topic "Help the environment by recycling paper" and deliver it to imagined different audiences: your friends, your boss, and young children, etc.

Are you good at adapting your message and delivering it to your audience?

6. Group Work

One of your team members is selected by the city government to be the city commissioner for tourism promotion. He/She is expected to make an attractive presentation to potential tourists. Help him/her gather materials and prepare the presentation. The class can act as the audience and then choose the best speaker.

Extra Input

Read the following speech excerpts carefully and see how they are well suited for the occasion and the audience.

William Faulkner: Nobel Prize Speech (1949)

I feel that this award was not made to me as a man, but to my work, a life's work in the agony and sweat of the human spirit. Not for glory and least of all, for profit, but to create out of the material of the human spirit something which did not exist before. So this award is only mine in trust.

I would like to... use this moment as a pinnacle from which I might be listened to by the young men and women, already dedicated to the same anguish and travail, among whom is already that one who will someday stand here where I am standing.

... the young man or woman writing today has forgotten the problems of the human heart in conflict with itself, which alone can make good writing because only that is worth writing about, worth the agony and the sweat.

He must learn them again; he must teach himself that the basest of all things is to be afraid, and teaching himself that, forget it forever, leaving no room in his workshop for anything but the old verities and truths of the heart. The old universal truths, lacking which any story is ephemeral and doomed: love and honor and pity and pride, and compassion and sacrifice...

Woodrow Wilson: *The Fourteen Points* (1918)

Gentlemen of the Congress,

We entered this war because violations of right had occurred which touched us to the quick and made the life of our own people impossible unless they were corrected and the world secured once for all against their recurrence.

What we demand in this war, therefore, is nothing peculiar to ourselves. It is that the world be made fit and safe to live in; and particularly that it be made safe for every peace-loving nation which, like our own, wishes to live its own life, determine its own institutions, be assured of justice and fair dealing by the other peoples of the world, as against force and selfish aggression.

All the peoples of the world are in effect partners in this interest, and for our own part we see very clearly that unless justice be done to others it will not be done to us.

... we feel ourselves to be intimate partners of all the governments and peoples associated together against the imperialists. We cannot be separated in interest or divided in purpose. We stand together until the end...

New Hurdles

1. Retelling

Listen to the passage and retell it immediately after you have heard it.

I saw *The Lion King* during my last trip to Broadway, and I absolutely loved it. Of course there were hundreds of children in attendance, some of them as young as 5 years old. It was all very cute and it was great to see so many kids at a Broadway show.

You simply can not have the same expectations from an audience at a Disney musical that you have at other adult-oriented shows. *The Lion King* is nearly three hours long, and you can not expect a 5-year-old to sit there in complete silence for that long. All things considered, I thought the youngsters at the show were very well behaved.

Still, I got kicked in the back of the seat a couple times and the kids on both sides of me were a little chatty. They used their indoor voices, but every few minutes a little voice would pipe up with questions — and they had lots of questions. "Who's that?" "Is he dead?" were a couple of the ones I remembered. I can not blame them. They were exactly the kind of questions I would have asked at their age if my parents had taken me to a Broadway show.

At intermission, I looked at the little boy who was kicking my seat. He was so cutely dressed that all I could do was smile. He couldn't have been more than 7 or 8, and he was with his grandparents. When I complimented him on his wardrobe, his grandmother sounded a little disappointed that he wasn't wearing a tie.

Yeah, the kicking and talking did get slightly annoying after a while, but it did not ruin my enjoyment of the show in the least. *The Lion King* is probably better when you see it with hundreds of kids. I mean, why would I want to see it with 1 500 cynical, bored adults like myself?

2. Talking on a Given Topic

In order to make more international friends, you are posting a personal ad on line to introduce yourself to foreigners. How can you introduce yourself properly so as to make friends with people from different cultures? Please give an oral presentation introducing yourself for this purpose. You have three minutes to prepare your talk and then talk to your partner.

3. Role Play

The task involves two students, Student A and Student B. Each has a specified role as follows. Although the situation is the same, your roles are different. Learn about the role you want to play. Your preparation time is three minutes. Your conversation is limited to four minutes.

Student A: Nowadays, due to the bleak employment situation, more students choose to continue their studies. You and your partner are discussing the issue. You think students should pursue their master's degree in a domestic university. Your partner does not agree. Try to convince him/her. Remember you should start the conversation.

Student B: Nowadays, due to the bleak employment situation, more students choose to continue their studies. You and your partner are discussing the issue. You think students should pursue their master's degree in a foreign university. Your partner does not agree. Try to convince him/her.

Notes

1. Dorothy Sarnoff (1914 — 2008): American singer, speech consultant, and author. She founded "Speech Dynamics Inc.", a speech consultancy firm, and held speech cosmetics classes in New York City. She was also considered a pioneer of the Self-Help Movement in the 20th century.

Amusement Park

1. Movie to Enjoy

See the following movie and share your personal view with your classmates next week.

Air Force One (1997)

This movie is a prominent symbol of the American presidency and its power. On the U.S. president's journey home after making a speech in Moscow, Russian hijackers took over the plane. However, as a former Medal of Honor winner, the president finally succeeded in regaining control of the plane and rescued his wife and daughter.

Special Highlight

The scene in which President Marshall delivers his surprise anti-terrorism speech is especially memorable.

Do you feel the power of the speech? How much can a politician achieve his political purposes through persuasive talks and speeches? Or how much is leadership built upon eloquence?

2. Song to Enjoy

The following is part of the lyrics to the song "Over the Rainbow" by Judy Garland. Find a recording of the song, listen to it and complete the lyrics.

Do you feel this song is particularly written for children? In what way does it try to appeal to its audience?

> Somewhere over the rainbow way up high
> There's a land that I heard of once in a lullaby
> Somewhere over the rainbow skies are blue
> And the dreams that you dare to dream really do come true
> Someday I wish upon a star
> And wake up where the clouds are far behind me
> Where troubles smelled like lemon drops
> Way above the chimney tops
> That's where you'll find me
> ...

3. Community Learning

The whole class is divided into several groups. Each is required to design a questionnaire on a specific speech topic and conduct a survey among students. Then each group should analyze the would-be audience according to the findings and results of the survey and prepare a relevant speech tailored to the needs of the audience. Choose a spokesperson to deliver the speech and other group members should assess the effectiveness of the speech.

Unit 19

Speech Topics and Plans

> Oral delivery aims at persuasion and making the listener believe they are converted. Few persons are capable of being convinced; the majority allow themselves to be persuaded.
> — Johann Wolfgang von Goethe[1]

Unit Goals

- To learn to select a topic and plan your speech properly
- To learn what the persuasive routes are
- To be able to apply the strategies to persuasive speeches

Warm-Up

1. Why do you think speech contests use very general topics such as "The future is now" or "Unity and diversity"?
2. When you come across a big topic, what do you usually do? Would you choose to narrow it down first or would you rather talk about it on a general, philosophical level?
3. Are you more comfortable with big topics, or are you more confident when dealing with a specific issue?

Knowledge Input

Speech Topics and Plans

Everyone learns how to persuade from their first days of life. You might be inherently able to use the art of persuasion and get your most wanted response. As you get older, you learn more sophisticated means of persuasion. Persuasive speech is the art of selecting topics, arranging content and words, and delivering soundly to influence the audience.

When faced with a speech topic, you need to be able to identify and define the main elements that the topic may cover, and then choose a specific aspect of the topic and apply it to your speech. In "reframing" the topic or limiting the scope, you should keep in view your audience and decide on the angle or aspect that will be of interest to them. Good speeches are often in tune with local interests, dealing with the hot topics on the calendar and current subjects in the market place.

Successful persuasion depends a lot on what aspect you choose to talk about, or in what specific way you choose to see the topic. So it is advisable to focus on an aspect that you feel strong about. Only when you feel committed to a subject yourself can you persuade powerfully.

When you find a group of students are speaking about the same topic, as in a speech contest or classroom presentation, you should try your best to be unique and interesting in the selection of a specific perspective. You can draw on your knowledge reserve, critical thinking ability and sense of humor in order to stand out as a different and interesting voice.

Once you have decided on what aspect to focus, you can go on to plan your speech carefully. This means that you should develop a central point (the purpose stated in your thesis statement) suited to the audience and occasions and plan structure and content to get your point through. In creating the speech, your writing techniques will come in handy to help you develop a unified, coherent, and clearly organized speech draft.

Since your audience hears the speech just once and has no opportunity to review what's been said, it is essential that you keep the organization simple and straightforward. The usual "introduction — body — conclusion" format will serve your speech very well. In the introduction part, you should arouse the audience's interest, reveal the topic and state your point clearly. The body part is the major content you generate to support your point. It is important to weave a wide variety of supporting materials into the speech, since various audience members may not be responsive to one kind of material but may be responsive to another. It is also suggested that the number of your sub-point should not be more than three, so as to keep your speech concise and clear. You should also arrange the sub-points in an order that can best serve your point. In the conclusion part, quickly round up your principal points and bring the speech to a natural, positive ending.

Apart from basic principles and techniques in writing, persuasive speeches also use special appealing strategies to get the most wanted response from the audience. We will discuss the use of the three appeals — rational, emotional and credibility — in the following units.

Knowledge Internalization

1. Pair Work

Look at the picture of "wearable paradigm". Discuss the following questions.

1) What aspects does the topic of "wearable paradigm" cover?

2) Take your partner as your audience and find out what aspects he/she is most interested in.

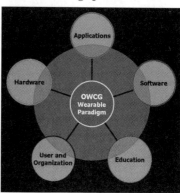

2. Solo Work

What qualities do you think will make a person successful? Please make a simple plan for your point. Your plan can be like an outline including a thesis statement, three sub-points and relevant supporting materials.

3. Group Work

The following are some hot topics. Study each one, and if necessary, do research work in order to understand them. Then each person should come up with a specific point concerning each topic. Share your point with your group members and widen each other's scope of understanding of the topics.

1) Green politics[2]
2) Chinese elements in fashion
3) Being a volunteer
4) Housing prices

Lexical Power Build-Up

1. Lexical Input

Transitional words and phrases provide logical organization and understandability, and improve the connections and transitions between thoughts when you are speaking on a topic. A coherent speech allows the audience to flow smoothly from the first point to the last. Here are some useful expressions for transition of ideas. Practice them until you can say them automatically.

1) *From general to specific*

especially, for instance, in particular, markedly, namely, particularly, including, specifically, such as, etc.

2) *From specific to general*

as a rule, as usual, for the most part, generally, generally speaking, ordinarily, usually, etc.

3) *Summarizing*

after all, all in all, all things considered, briefly, by and large, in any case, in any event, in brief, in conclusion, on the whole, in short, in summary, in the final analysis, in the long run, to sum up, to summarize, etc.

4) *Cause and effect*

accordingly, as a result, consequently, for this reason, for this purpose, hence, otherwise, so then, subsequently, therefore, thus, thereupon, etc.

5) *Restatement or paraphrasing*

in essence, in other words, namely, that is, that is to say, in short, in brief, to put it differently, etc.

2. Pair Work

Work with your partner and try to add more words and expressions to the lists above. Then share your findings with the class.

3. Group Work

Besides the above-listed "relationships" between ideas, what other relationships are there? Find out more relationships between ideas and their transitions. Then share your findings with the class.

Comprehensive Input

Below is an excerpt of Chinese Premier Wen Jiabao's speech at the University of Cambridge, February 2, 2009.

I stress the importance of seeing China in the light of her development, because the world is changing and China is changing. China is no longer the closed and backward society it was 100 years ago, or the poor and ossified society 30 years ago. What the Beijing Olympic Games showcased is a colorful China, both ancient and modern. I

therefore encourage you to visit China more often and see more places there. This way, you will better understand what the Chinese people are thinking and doing, and what they are interested in. You will get to know the true China, a country constantly developing and changing. You will also better appreciate how China has been tackling the ongoing global financial crisis.

This unprecedented financial crisis has inflicted a severe impact on both China and Britain as well as other European countries. The crisis has not yet hit the bottom, and it is hard to predict what further damage it may cause. To work together and tide over the difficulties has become our top priority.

I believe that closer cooperation is needed to meet the global crisis, and the level of cooperation hinges upon the level of mutual trust. The Chinese government maintains that countries should: first and foremost, run their own affairs well and refrain from shifting troubles onto others; second, carry out cooperation with full sincerity and avoid pursuing one's own interests at the expense of others; and third, address both the symptoms and the root cause of the problem. A palliative approach will not work. We should not treat only the head when the head aches, and the foot when the foot hurts. As I reiterated at the World Economic Forum Annual Meeting in Davos, necessary reform of the international monetary and financial systems should be carried out to establish a new international financial order that is fair, equitable, inclusive and well-managed. We should create an institutional environment conducive to global economic growth...

Comprehensive Practice

1. Solo Work

Read the speech aloud to your classmates. Make sure you use appropriate speed, stress and pauses to enable your audience to understand what you are saying.

2. Pair Work

Study this speech and try to answer the following questions.
1) What aspect of China does this speech focus on? Why so?
2) What is the function of the first paragraph?
3) What is the main idea of this part of the speech?
4) How are the ideas connected with each other? Is the logic and connection clear enough?

3. Solo Work

In terms of topic selection and speech planning, what do you think you can learn from this speech?

4. Solo Work

Use one of the four topics and compose a 3-minute speech with a focused area of interest and a central point.
1) Green politics
2) Chinese elements in fashion
3) Being a volunteer

4) Housing prices

5. Group Work

Deliver your speech in your group and ask your group members to give suggestions for improvement. Rehearse the delivery again. Each group should choose the best speaker to present the speech to the class.

6. Class Work

Hold a 20-minute debate on the topic "Advertising plays a negative role in society". Both sides should plan three sub-points and find supporting materials from credible sources to support your stand. After the debate, review your performance and see which side plans better and which side delivers better.

Extra Input

Read the following short speeches and learn how the speaker made his points concise, clear, and effective.

Second Inaugural Address
George Washington

Fellow Citizens,

I am again called upon by the voice of my country to execute the functions of its Chief Magistrate. When the occasion proper for it shall arrive, I shall endeavor to express the high sense I entertain of this distinguished honor, and of the confidence which has been reposed in me by the people of united America.

Previous to the execution of any official act of the President the Constitution requires an oath of office. This oath I am now about to take, and in your presence: That if it shall be found during my administration of the Government I have in any instance violated willingly or knowingly the injunctions thereof, I may, besides incurring constitutional punishment, be subject to the upbraiding of all who are now witnesses of the present solemn ceremony.

(Delivered on March 4, 1793)

Two Americas
John Edwards

I stand here tonight ready to work with you to make America stronger. And we have much work to do, because the truth is, we still live in a country where there are two different Americas — one for all of those people who have lived the American dream and do not have to worry, and another for most Americans, everybody else who struggle to make ends meet every single day…

We can build one America where we no longer have two health care systems: one for families who get the best health care money can buy, and then one for everybody else rationed out by insurance companies, drug companies, HMOs...

We shouldn't have two public school systems in this country: one for the most affluent communities, and one for everybody else. None of us believe that the quality of a child's education should be controlled by where they live or the affluence of the community they live in...

We shouldn't have two different economies in America: one for people who are set for life, they know their kids and their grand-kids are going to be just fine; and then one for most Americans, people who live paycheck to paycheck...

(Delivered on July 28, 2004)

New Hurdles

1. Retelling

Listen to the passage and retell it immediately after you have heard it.

Being inspired and motivated by the movie *Pay It Forward*, I came up with the topic of today's speech. I hope that after listening to my speech today, my audiences can slow down their pace, watch people more, show their concern and help those who are in need with a little more warmth and care that originate from the bottom of our heart.

I think that most in my audience have seen the movie *Pay It Forward* and must have been touched by the actions the main character took and the great influence he produced. He believed deeply in the goodness of human nature and was determined to change the world for the better. His faith and determination enabled him to succeed. Thus, I would like to tell my audiences that we can also do the same things that he did in the movie, paying our love to people around us and spread it to the world.

In my speech, I will relate to the movie and let my audience see why we need to "pay it forward" rather than "pay it back" when someone does us a favor. In addition, I will take myself as an example, offering my own experiences of actively helping others to deepen my audiences' understanding of my point. By showing them the joy of caring for and helping others, I will try to move them action to change the world with love.

My conclusion would be this: although we may be sometimes disappointed at indifference at large in the world, and feel hopeless about the conflicts and wars that are going on, a little drop of love may make our day bright, that is, as long as we believe in the magic of love.

2. Talking on a Given Topic

Some people argue that the cloning of human beings should be banned by law. What do you think about it? You have three minutes to prepare your talk and then talk to your partner.

3. Role Play

The task involves two students, Student A and Student B. Each has a specified role as follows. Although the situation is the same, your roles are different. Learn about the role you want to play. Your preparation time is three minutes. Your conversation is limited to four minutes.

Student A: Today in China, the number of college students using credit cards is increasing. You and your partner are discussing the issue. You think by owning a credit card, a college student can learn how to budget and even finance. Your partner does not agree. Try to convince him/her. Remember you should start the conversation.

Student B: Today in China, the number of college students using credit cards is increasing. You and your partner are discussing the issue. You do not think this should be encouraged because college students tend to spend money on impulse and too much overdrawing may leave the student a bad credit record. Your partner does not agree. Try to convince him/her.

Notes

1. Johann Wolfgang von Goethe (1749 — 1832): German playwright, poet, novelist and dramatist.
2. Green politics is a political idea that places a great importance on ecological and environmental goals. Green politics is advocated by supporters of the Green movement, which has been active through Green parties in many nations since the early 1980s.

Amusement Park

1. Movie to Enjoy

See the following movie and share your personal view with your classmates.

The American President (**1995**)

The American President is a romantic comedy. In the film, President Andrew Shepherd (Michael Douglas) is a widower who pursues a relationship with attractive lobbyist Sydney Ellen Wade. Their relationship opens the door for his prime political opponent, Senator Bob Rumson, to launch an attack on the President's character, something he could not do in the previous election as Shepherd's wife had only recently died …

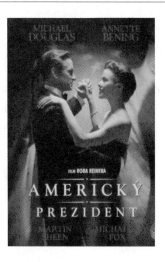

Special Highlight

Highly recommended is the president's final speech in the film when he finally attacks the character of the Republican presidential candidate, Sen. Bob Rumson.

Do you think romance and power are mixed and matched well in this film? What do you think is the connection between power and romance?

2. Song to Enjoy

The following is part of the lyrics to the song "This Land Is Our Land" by The Brothers Four. Find a recording of the song, listen to it and complete the lyrics.

Think about what emotions are expressed in this song. How do the lyrics echo the emotions?

This land is your land
This land is my land
From California to the New York island
From the redwood forest to the Gulf Stream
This land was made for you and me

As I was walking that ribbon of highway
I saw above me that endless skyway
I saw below me that golden valley
This land was made for you and me

I've roamed and rambled
And I followed my footsteps
To the sparkling sands of her diamond deserts
And all around me a voice was sounding
This land was made for you and me
…

3. Community Learning

In groups of four assigned by your teacher, select four topics related to effective business communication or some other business-related topic. A group leader may randomly assign a topic to each member or allow the members to select a topic. Following a brief preparation time, each member will give a one-to-two-minute presentation to the group. After all the presentations are given, the group will briefly discuss the strengths and weaknesses of each report and attempt to provide each member with a few specific suggestions for improvement.

Unit 20

Logos — Rational Appeal

> The intuitive mind is a sacred gift and the rational mind is a faithful servant. We have created a society that honors the servant and has forgotten the gift.
> — Albert Einstein

Unit Goals

- To learn what logos or rational appeal is
- To learn the elements of rational appeal
- To apply rational appeal to persuasive speeches

Warm-Up

1. Would you explain the meaning of "rational"? Can you give any examples of being rational?
2. Suppose you were a doctor, how would you describe a body? If you were an artist, how would you do it?

Knowledge Input

Rational Appeal

Persuasive speech is like a demonstration. When a speaker addresses an audience, he/she must use certain modes of persuasion. They are devices in rhetoric that classify the speaker's appeal to the audience. As is mentioned in Aristotle's *On Rhetoric*, persuasion is achieved by the speaker's *personal character* (ethos) when the speech is so spoken as to make us think him credible, may come through the hearers when the *speech stirs their emotions* (pathos), and is effected through the *speech itself* when we have rationally proved a truth by means of the persuasive arguments suitable to the case in question (logos). Deciding how to best use the three modes of ethos, pathos and logos helps to build up a speaker's unique rhetorical stance.

Logos was first given special attention in ancient Greek philosophy when it was mentioned by Heraclitus, who seemed not to use it in a special technical sense, while sophists used the term to mean discourse. Aristotle applied logos to rational discourse, from which the term *logic* is derived. Logos normally implies *numbers, polls, and other mathematical or scientific data*, so it is harder to argue against a logos argument since data is hard to manipulate. It also makes the speaker look prepared and knowledgeable to the audience, enhancing ethos. Actually, logos is likely to be misleading or inaccurate, for data can be confusing and thus confuse the audience. As was said by Mark Twain, there are liars, darn liars and statisticians.

However, though it is possible for a liar to misuse pathos to play on an audience's heartstrings, his rhetoric must stand or fall on their own rational merits once the audience is also trained in logic. *Induction and deduction* both play a big role. Induction means a type of specific-to-general reasoning and an example-based argument, which attempt to establish something about the future. Deduction is a type of general-to-specific reasoning and a generalized argument. The speaker usually takes the general rule and then tries to show how a specific example fits into that larger category. Deductive reasoning builds layer upon layer of proof, then comes to a conclusion that can be tested. Inductive reasoning is somewhat trickier and can lead to fallacious reasoning. Where deductive reasoning can be represented as a pyramid, inductive reasoning flips the pyramid over and is used to draw a broad range of conclusions based on a single point of evidence.

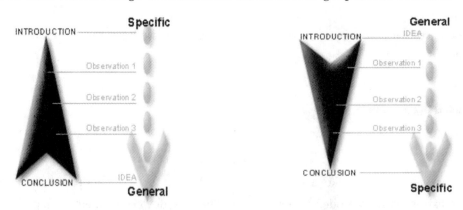

Logos or rational appeal is a strategic application of logic, claims, and evidence to convince an audience of a certain point. A successful application is always due to strong and clear claims, reasonable qualifiers, valid warrants, clear reasons, strong evidence (facts, statistics, personal experience, expert authority, interviews, observations, anecdotes, testimonies, etc.), and acknowledgement of the opposition, etc. When poorly used, rational appeals might include over-generalized claims, reasons that are not fully explained or supported, logical fallacies, evidence misused or ignored, and no recognition of opposing views, etc. For example, a speaker urging college students to boycott soda machines on campus because of the high sugar and high caffeine content of the drinks would seek information on the negative effects of sugar and caffeine on the human body as one part of the speech. If the speaker finds out that some sugar and some caffeine can actually benefit a college student's classroom performance, then it is important to define the difference between some intake and excessive intake. That may take some additional research, but that's part of the speaker's responsibility.

Knowledge Internalization

1. Pair Work

Discuss the following questions with your partner after reading the text.

1) How often do you practice rational appeal in your speech? Please give us some examples.
2) It's said that the world is littered with statistics, which are likely to be misleading or inaccurate. What's your understanding of statistics? And how could you improve your rational appeals with them?
3) What should a speaker do in order to acquire a variety of credible evidence to prove his/her point?

2. Group Work

Form groups of four or five. Each person should give an example of induction and deduction. Then share your examples with your group. Choose the best examples in your group and share them with your class.

3. Solo Work

You know you should avoid logical fallacies in order to present effective rational appeal. Get to know some often-committed fallacious reasoning such as hasty generalization, post hoc, bandwagon, etc. Remember that you need to steer clear of such fallacies whenever you are trying to prove a point.

4. Group Work

In Western cultures and modern East Asia, the *I Ching* is sometimes regarded as a system of symbolism. The classic consists of a series of symbols, rules for manipulating these symbols, poems, and commentary. Please launch a team research on *I Ching* and make a rational presentation in your class.

Lexical Power Build-Up

1. Input

Here are some ways of using rational appeal.

1) *Numbers*

To quote statistics: Statistics show that we went from the 16-bit processor with a meg of memory to the 286 that gave us a 24-bit memory space, then to the 386 with a 32-bit memory space, and now we're in the transition to 64-bit.

To quote sources: The most recent surveys done by medical institutions around the country say that each year Australia see 18 000 new diagnoses of prostate cancer, which kills 3 000 men.

To estimate/predict: It's estimated that there will be over 20 000 students studying at this school.

2) *Theories and authoritative opinion*

To begin with a theory: According to Smith's prescription of letting markets prevail with minimal governmental interference…

To insert a theory. With the continuing progress of miniaturization — driven by Moore's Law — it is now possible to create tiny devices that can sense their environment in a variety of ways,…

3) *Classification and exemplification*

To classify: Beyond deregulation, innovative technologies, especially information technologies, have…

To illustrate: An example of this new partnership-based relationship is Thomson Trade Web's flexible business model to reward dealers,…

2. Solo Work

Reconstruct the examples in Lexical Power Build-Up with new information.

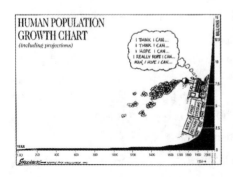

3. Group Work

Look at the chart reflecting the world population. Please work in teams talking about what is implied in this chart. Use the expressions you've learned and then share your findings with your classmates.

4. Group Work

As is known, the solar system consists of the sun

and those celestial objects bound to it by gravity, including the eight planets. Please do team research on the solar system and choose a spokesperson for your group to deliver a presentation on your research findings.

Comprehensive Input

Below are the U. S. Federal Reserve Chairman Ben Bernanke's remarks in the early period of 2009, just following the worldwide financial tsunami initiating in late 2008. According to Associated Press, Bernanke was a bit more optimistic in his latest speech.

Fiscal policy can stimulate economic activity, but a sustained recovery will also require a comprehensive plan to stabilize the financial system. (Jan. 13)

I hope the recession will end this year, but that there were significant risks to that forecast. Any economic turnaround will hinge on the success of the Fed and the Obama administration in getting credit and financial markets to operate more normally again. (Feb. 24)

I acknowledge the recession is more severe than the Fed had expected. Still, there's a good chance the recession could end this year if the government managed to get financial markets to operate more normally again. First, we must address the problem of financial institutions that are deemed too big — or perhaps too interconnected — to fail. Second, we must strengthen what I will call the financial infrastructure — the systems, rules, and conventions that govern trading, payment, clearing, and settlement in financial markets — to ensure that it will perform well under stress. Third, we should review regulatory policies and accounting rules to ensure that they do not overly magnify the ups and downs in the financial system and the economy. Finally, we should consider whether the creation of an authority specifically charged with monitoring and addressing systemic risks would help protect the system from financial crises like the one we are currently experiencing. (March 10)

These are extraordinarily challenging times for our financial system and our economy. I am confident that we can meet these challenges, not least because I have great confidence in the underlying strengths of the American economy. For its part, the Federal Reserve will make responsible use of all its tools to stabilize financial markets and institutions, to promote the extension of credit to creditworthy borrowers, and to help build a foundation for economic recovery. Over the long term, we also look forward to working with our counterparts at other supervisory and regulatory agencies in the United States and around the world to address the structural issues that have led to this crisis so as to minimize the risk of ever facing such a situation again. (April 3)

Recently there have been tentative signs that the sharp decline in economic activity may be slowing, for example, in data on home sales, homebuilding, and consumer spending, including sales of new motor vehicles. A leveling out of economic activity is the first step toward recovery. To be sure, we will not have a sustainable recovery without a stabilization of our financial system and credit markets. We are making progress on that front as well, and the Federal Reserve is committed to working to restore financial stability as a necessary step toward full economic recovery. (April 14)

Comprehensive Practice

1. Solo Work

Consider why Associated Press thought Bernanke's latest remark a bit more optimistic.

2. Pair Work

Discuss the following questions with your partner.
1) What supporting materials are used for rational appeal?
2) What logical pattern is used to realize rational appeal?
3) What effect do such appeals reach?

3. Class Work

Do some research work and try to find more evidence for Bernanke's claim.

4. Pair Work

Talk about your career plan with your partner and try to help each other improve his/her vision rationally.

5. Solo Work

Deliver a two-minute mini-speech using rational appeal to prove or disprove the following claims.
1) Global warming is the major cause of more frequent and extreme weather all over the world.
2) Planning is more important than action in trying to achieve a goal.

6. Group Work

Debate on the topic: The opportunity cost of attending graduate school is too high for college students.

Try to achieve rational appeal through the use of credible statistics and other evidence to defend your stand and attack the opposing stand.

Extra Input

The following are two excerpts of sample speeches using rational appeals. Study the excerpts carefully and find out how the speakers practice their rational appeal techniques.

We Can Still Win the Euro Referendum (Excerpt)
Roy Jenkins, June 2000

The lessons I draw from this experience, in which I was President of the Britain in Europe "yes" campaign, and from the other pieces of history I have cited, are the following:

First, it is the most idle dream to think that Britain can be a leading player in Europe so long as it does not participate in Europe's main thrust at the moment, which is the Euro. Eleven of the 15 member states are already in. One (Greece) is about to join. Two (Sweden and, a little more doubtfully, Denmark) are moving hard and ahead of us in this direction. To imagine that in a community where 14 countries could be in and one is out, the 14 will look to the one for leadership is manifest nonsense.

Second, a Euro referendum must not be long delayed after the coming general election. If it is, Germany, France and the other core members will conclude that we will always hover on the brink, and will settle their minds firmly on going ahead without us, which indeed they are already showing signs of doing.

Third, a successful pro Euro referendum campaign must be fought on a cross-party basis, as was that of 1975. But, more than this, it must be more than an opportunistic alliance of suspicion and maneuver. It must be done with mutual confidence and even a little love. That again was achieved in 1975. My mind retains a particularly vivid memory of one satisfactory meeting. It was in Norwich on the penultimate evening of the campaign. I shared the platform with Willie Whitelaw and David Steel. The British public showed every sign of liking the spectacle of politicians co-operating for a cause in which they believed rather than hurling routine insults at each other across the floor of the Commons.

...

With a properly conducted campaign, a referendum in 2001 can be won. But the government is leaving it dangerously late to start throwing its weight behind a strong, positive case.

The Time Has Come for Universal Health Care (Excerpt)

Barack Obama, Jan. 2007

You know the statistics. Family premiums are up by nearly 87% over the last five years, growing five times faster than workers' wages. Deductibles are up 50%. Co-payments for care and prescriptions are through the roof.

Nearly 11 million Americans who are already insured spent more than a quarter of their salary on health care last year. And over half of all family bankruptcies today are caused by medical bills.

But they say it's too costly to act.

Almost half of all small businesses no longer offer health care to their workers, and so many others have responded to rising costs by laying off workers or shutting their doors for good. Some of the biggest corporations in America, giants of industry like GM and Ford, are watching foreign competitors based in countries with universal health care run circles around them, with a GM car containing twice as much health care cost as a Japanese car.

But they say it's too risky to act.

They tell us it's too expensive to cover the uninsured, but they do not mention that every time an American without health insurance walks into an emergency room, we pay even more. Our family's premiums are $922 higher because of the cost of care for the uninsured.

We pay $15 billion more in taxes because of the cost of care for the uninsured. And it's trapped us in a vicious cycle. As the uninsured cause premiums to rise, more employers drop coverage. As more employers drop coverage, more people become uninsured, and premiums rise even further.

But the skeptics tell us that reform is too costly, too risky, too impossible for America.

Well the skeptics must be living somewhere else. Because when you see what the health care crisis is doing to our families, to our economy, to our country, you realize that caution is what's costly. Inaction is what's risky. Doing nothing is what's impossible when it comes to health care in America.

It's time to act. This isn't a problem of money. This is a problem of will. A failure of leadership. We already spend $2.2 trillion a year on health care in this country. My colleague, Senator Ron Wyden, who's recently developed a bold new health care plan of his own, tells it this way:

For the money Americans spent on health care last year, we could have hired a group of skilled physicians, paid each one of them $200 000 to care for just seven families, and guaranteed every single American quality, affordable health care…

New Hurdles

1. Retelling

Listen to the passage and retell it immediately after you have heard it.

I am sure that my first thought, when I received the call telling me that I would receive the Prize in Economic Sciences, was the same as the first thought of many previous recipients — namely, to wonder which of my colleagues had arranged this elaborate practical joke.

Eventually, however, the awesome reality sank in — and what I felt was not pride but a sense of astonished humility.

My thanks go out, in this wonderful moment, to those who made it possible — to my wife, to my parents, and, not least, to my colleagues around the world.

The great economist John Maynard Keynes once wrote of the foolish things a man thinking alone can temporarily come to believe. Fortunately, I did not have to think alone: the creation of the modern theory of international trade and economic geography was very much a collective effort. The new ideas were hammered out over years of conferences and correspondence involving men and women from many countries. This group of men and women constituted one of history's great invisible colleges, and together we made a revolution in the way economists think about the most fundamental aspects of the global economy.

So let me express my deepest gratitude to the Economics Prize Committee for recognizing this work, and for honoring my own part in the achievement. It's an honor that I will spend the rest of my life trying to live up to. Thank you.

(Paul Krugman's speech at the Nobel Banquet, Dec. 10, 2008)

2. Talking on a Given Topic

You are required to give a talk to tell how to find materials and evidence for rational appeal. You have three minutes to prepare your talk and then talk to your partner.

3. Role Play

The task involves two students, Student A and Student B. Each has a specified role as follows. Although the situation is the same, your roles are different. Learn about the role you want to play. Your preparation time is three minutes. Your conversation is limited to four minutes.

Student A: Job hunters who attended the first job fair for Chinese overseas students in Beijing were disappointed to learn that most of the enterprises only offered about 3 000 yuan, or about $ 400 a month, about the same salary as for domestic college graduates. You think that the proposed salary is too low considering the costs involved in studying abroad and more importantly, these students have learned advanced skills. Your partner does not agree. Try to convince him/her. Remember you should start the conversation.

Student B: Job hunters who attended the first job fair for Chinese overseas students in Beijing were disappointed to learn that most of the enterprises only offered about 3 000 Yuan, or about $400 a month, about the same salary as for domestic college graduates. You do not think that the proposed salary is too low because returned Chinese overseas students do not actually have many advantages, especially those who only studied one or two years overseas with the support of their parents and lived an extravagant life there. Your partner does not agree. Try to convince him/her.

Amusement Park

1. Movie to Enjoy

See the following movie and share your personal view with your classmates next week.

The Pursuit of Happyness (2006)

Christopher Gardner has invested heavily in a "Bone Density Scanner", an apparatus twice as expensive as an x-ray with practically the same resolution. However, he failed in the business, followed by some further strikes. Forced to live out on the streets with his son, Gardner is now desperate to find a steady job. He takes on a job as a stockbroker, but before he can receive pay, he needs to go through 6 months of training, and to sell his devices...

Special Highlight

One touching scene in the movie is when Chris Gardner gets hired after the internship and he seems to be able to finally be happy. In real life, Chris still had many challenges, especially in starting his own firm in Chicago.

What does the movie tell you about the meaning of happiness? Why do you think in the title of the movie, the word "happyness" is misspelled?

2. Song to Enjoy

The following is part of the lyrics to the song "Let's Talk about Love" by Celine Dion. Find a recording of the song, listen to it and complete the lyrics.

Everywhere I go all the places that I've been
Every smile's a new horizon on a land I've never seen
There are people around the world
Different faces, different names
But there's one true emotion that reminds me we're the same...
Let's talk about love

From the laughter of a child to the tears of a grown man
There's a thread that runs right through us and helps us understand
As subtle as a breeze — that fans a flicker to a flame
From the very first sweet melody to the very last refrain

...

3. Community Learning

The whole class is divided into groups of four or five to discuss whether information technology dominates or facilitates people's lives. Each group is expected to use rhetoric techniques to persuade others. The audience will judge each group's proposal and ask each speaker relevant questions to test his/her credibility.

Unit 21

Pathos — Emotional Appeal

> Whenever you find humor, you find pathos close by his side.
>
> — Edwin P. Whipple[1]

Unit Goals

- To learn what pathos or emotional appeal is
- To learn the elements of emotional appeal
- To apply emotional appeal to persuasive speeches

Warm-Up

1. Have you ever bought any products because you had been impressed and convinced by their advertisements? In what way does the advertisement affect you, rationally or emotionally?

2. If you are introducing your hometown to your friends, you may use facts and figures to make your introduction truthful and reliable. But if you are to tell your friends about your love for your hometown, are you going to do the same thing? What differences do you think there might be?
3. Do you know what a metaphor is? If you don't, look it up and find some examples. What effects does a metaphor create?

Knowledge Input

Emotional Appeal

Emotional appeal, also known as pathos, is to use the manipulation of the audience's emotions, rather than valid logic, to win an argument. It can be in the form of metaphor, simile, a passionate delivery, or even a simple claim that a matter is unjust. Not surprisingly, emotional appeal targets the emotions of the audience to create some kind of connection between the speaker and the audience. It can be particularly powerful if used well, and most effective when the speaker connects with an underlying value of the audience.

The most powerful speakers and speeches in history always used emotional appeal. To the advantages of the emotions, Quintilian[2] argued "profits may induce the judges to regard our case as superior to that of our opponent, but the appeal to the emotions will do more, for it will make them wish our case to be better. And what they wish, they will also believe."

A classic example of emotional appeal in romance is found in Jane Austen's *Pride and Prejudice.* Mr. Darcy persuades Elizabeth to reconsider her disposition of him through emotional appeal in his letter when he informs her of Mr. Wickham's offenses. Another example of emotional appeal used in speech is Martin Luther King's *I Have a Dream.* As we listen to the speech, we can hear the roaring cheers and feel the deep emotions flowing

through the crowd. The thundering voice of "I have a dream that one day ..." identifies his dreams and ideals with the audience. Therefore he successfully built up the emotional connection with the audience through sharing a dream with them.

Emotional appeal could be accomplished either by using a metaphor or a story, or by general passion in the delivery and an overall number of emotional items in the text of the speech. Emotional appeal could be a powerful strategy in persuasion through using strong imagery and symbols. Actually, it is sometimes misused intentionally to mislead an audience or to hide an argument that is weak in rational appeal. Once applied improperly, emotional appeal might become a substitute for logic and reason, such as using stereotypes to pit one group of people against another, offering an unthinking reaction to a complex problem, or taking advantage of emotions (through fear, hate, pity, prejudice, embarrassment, lust, or other feelings) to manipulate rather than convince credibly. As a result, many emotional appeals that are effective are credible, but there are also many that are not.

Good speakers should use credible emotional appeals together with strong evidence and reasoning in order to persuade or influence the audience. If they are only eager to sway their audience emotionally and rely more on the affective mode, emotional appeal is overdone.

Emotional appeal targets attitudes and values as a means of making human connections between the topic and the audience. Speakers want the audience to identify with the emotions and feelings evoked deliberately in the speech as a means of agreeing with them. A sound emotional appeal should possess the features of a fair manner presentation, rational appeal reinforcement, humanized diction and imagery and a balanced appeal to idealism, beauty, humor, nostalgia, pity, etc. People still need to do research and support contentions with evidence, and any appeal should engage the emotions of the audience as well.

Knowledge Internalization

1. Pair Work

Discuss the following questions with your partner after reading the text.
1) Why is emotional appeal effective in persuasion?
2) In what ways can we use emotional appeal in a speech?
3) Does emotional appeal mean the speaker gets emotional himself/herself? What is a sound emotional appeal like?
4) Does emotional appeal rule out rational appeal or do they reinforce each other? In what ways?

2. Pair Work

Aristotle pointed out that "our judgments when we are pleased and friendly are not the same as when we are pained and hostile". How do you understand this statement? Think it over and then present your ideas in a two-minute mini-presentation to your partner.

3. Group Work

In the Bible, there are many metaphors applied for emotional appeals, which in return tell the readers some valuable philosophies. Do some research on the emotional appeals in the

Bible and share your findings with your classmates.

Lexical Power Build-Up

1. Input

Here are some useful rhetorical methods for emotional appeal.

1) *Using metaphor*

A *bird* in the hand is worth two in the bush.

The Negro must boldly throw off *the manacles of self-abnegation* and say to himself and to the world, "I am somebody. I am a person. I am a man with dignity and honor."

Let us be dissatisfied until America will no longer have *a high blood pressure of creeds* and *an anemia of deeds*.

In treating an *ideological or a political malady*, one must never be rough and rash but must adopt the approach of "curing the sickness to save the patient".

One hundred years later, the Negro lives on *a lonely island of poverty* in the midst of *a vast ocean of material prosperity*.

From Stettin in the Baltic to Trieste in the Adriatic, *an iron curtain* has descended across the continent.

2) *Using image and symbol*

Reach for *your peak, your goal, your prize*.

You know some *birds* are not meant to be caged; *their feathers are just too bright*.

A *closed mouth* catches no *flies*.

Darkness cannot put out darkness. Only *light* can do that.

3) *Using emotional words*

We are fighting for freedom *for our children* every bit as much as in any war we've ever been in.

There is *the greatest danger* for the United States of America.

I see them guarding *their homes*, where *maidens* laugh and *children* play, where their *mothers and wives pray*.

Behind all this *storm*, I see that small group of *villainous men* who planned, organized and launched this *cataract of horrors* upon *mankind*.

2. Group Work

Read the following excerpt from Martin Luther King's speech "Where do we go from here" and point out the language features of emotional appeal.

...*It will give us the courage to face the uncertainties of the future. It will give our tired feet new strength as we continue our forward stride toward the city of freedom. When our days become dreary with low hovering clouds of despair, and when our nights* become darker than a thousand midnights, let us remember that there is a creative force in this universe, working to pull down the gigantic mountains of evil, a power that is able to make a way out of no way and transform dark yesterdays into bright tomorrows. Let us realize the arc of the moral universe is long but it bends toward justice.

Let us realize that William Cullen Bryant is right: "Truth crushed to earth will rise again." Let us go out realizing that the Bible is right: "Be not deceived. God is not mocked. Whatsoever a man soweth, that shall he also reap." This is our hope for the future, and with this faith we will be able to sing in some not too distant tomorrow with a cosmic past tense, "We have overcome, we have overcome, deep in my heart, I did believe we would overcome."

3. Solo Work

Try to rewrite some sentences in your previous speeches, using emotional appeal. Then compare the effectiveness of the two versions.

Comprehensive Input

U. S. President George W. Bush addressed Congress and the Nation on Thursday, September 21, 2001 concerning the terrorist attack on the World Trade Center in New York City and on the Pentagon building in Washington D. C. It was an outstanding speech, delivered with emotion and conviction. Journalists and historians have rated it as one of the greatest speeches ever made.

George W. Bush's Address to Congress
on 9/11/2001 Terrorist Attack (Excerpt)

In the normal course of events, Presidents come to this chamber to report on the state of the Union. Tonight, no such report is needed. It has already been delivered by the American people.

We have seen it in the courage of passengers, who rushed to save others on the

ground...We have seen the state of our Union in the endurance of rescuers, working past exhaustion. We have seen the unfurling of flags, the lighting of candles, and the giving of blood, the saying of prayers — in English, Hebrew, and Arabic. We have seen the decency of a loving and giving people, who have made the grief of strangers their own.

My fellow citizens, for the last nine days, the entire world has seen for itself the state of our Union and it is strong.

Tonight we are a country awakened to danger and called to defend freedom. Our grief has turned to anger, and anger to resolution. Whether we bring our enemies to justice, or bring justice to our enemies, justice will be done...

Americans are asking: How will we fight and win this war?

...We will direct every resource at our command — every means of diplomacy, every tool of intelligence, every instrument of law enforcement, every financial influence, and every necessary weapon of war — to the disruption and defeat of the global terror network ...We will starve terrorists of funding, turn them one against another, drive them from place to place, until there is no refuge or rest. And we will pursue nations that provide aid or safe haven to terrorism...

This is not, however, just America's fight. And what is at stake is not just America's freedom. This is the world's fight. This is civilization's fight. This is the fight of all who believe in progress and pluralism, tolerance and freedom.

The civilized world is rallying to America's side. They understand that if this terror goes unpunished, their own cities, their own citizens may be next. Terror, unanswered, can not only bring down buildings, it can threaten the stability of legitimate governments. And we will not allow it...

Americans are asking: What is expected of us?

I ask you to live your lives and hug your children. I know many citizens have fears tonight, and I ask you to be calm and resolute, even in the face of a continuing threat.

I ask you to uphold the values of America, and remember why so many have come here. We are in a fight for our principles, and our first responsibility is to live by them. No one should be singled out for unfair treatment or unkind words because of their ethnic background or religious faith.

...

Comprehensive Practice

1. Pair Work

Work with your partner and try to identify the emotional appeals in the sample speech.

2. Group Work

The use of figures of speech, such as parallelism, repetition, antithesis and rhetorical questions, can often lend strength to language. Work in a group and do research work on the figures of speech and then try to identify the figures of speech used in the sample.

3. Pair Work

How do you feel about the sample speech? How would it affect you if you were an audience member? Tell your partner your emotional response to the speech.

4. Solo Work

Compose a short persuasive speech based on one of the following topics. Use both rational and emotional appeal in your speech.

1) Helping physically handicapped children
2) Saving our city from pollution
3) What is patriotism?
4) Lifelong learning

5. Pair Work

Choose a simple poem and read it to your partner with emotions. Control your voice, pitch and tone when you read it.

6. Class Work

Deliver the speech your have composed to your class. The class should give each speaker adequate feedback on the speaker's use of appeals and delivery skills.

Extra Input

The following is the famous *Gettysburg Address* by Abraham Lincoln. This speech was delivered at the site of the bloody July 1-3, 1863 Civil War battle in Gettysburg, Pennsylvania. Emotional appeal was practiced well in the speech to show the president's feelings about the war and the nation.

Four score and seven years ago our fathers brought forth on this continent, a new nation, conceived in liberty, and dedicated to the proposition that all men are created equal.

Now we are engaged in a great civil war, testing whether that nation, or any nation so conceived and so dedicated, can long endure. We are met on a great battle-field of that war. We have come to dedicate a portion of that field, as a final resting place for those who here gave their lives that that nation might live. It is altogether fitting and proper that we should do this.

But, in a larger sense, we cannot dedicate — we cannot consecrate — we cannot hallow — this ground. The brave men, living and dead, who struggled here, have consecrated it, far above our poor power to add or detract. The world will little note, nor long remember what we say here, but it can never forget what they did here. It is for us the living, rather, to be dedicated here to the unfinished work which they who fought here have thus far so nobly advanced. It is rather for us to be here dedicated to the great task remaining before us — that from these honored dead we take increased devotion to that cause for which they gave the last full measure of devotion — that we here highly resolve that these dead shall not have died in vain — that this nation, under God, shall have a new birth of freedom — and that government of the people, by the people, for the people, shall not perish from the earth.

New Hurdles

1. Retelling

Listen to the passage and retell it immediately after you have heard it.

Fans, for the past two weeks you have been reading about what a bad break I got. Yet today I consider myself the luckiest man on the face of the earth. I have been in ballparks for seventeen years and have never received anything but kindness and encouragement from you fans.

Look at these grand men. Which of you would not consider it the highlight of his career to associate with them for even one day?

Sure, I'm lucky. Who would not consider it an honor to have known Jacob Ruppert — also the builder of baseball's greatest empire, Ed Barrow — to have spent the next nine years with that wonderful little fellow Miller Huggins — then to have spent the next nine years with that outstanding leader, that smart student of psychology — the best manager in baseball today, Joe McCarthy!

Sure, I'm lucky. When the New York Giants, a team you would give your right arm to beat, and vice versa, sends you a gift, that's something! When everybody down to the groundskeepers and those boys in white coats remember you with trophies, that's something.

When you have a wonderful mother-in-law who takes sides with you in squabbles against her own daughter, that's something. When you have a father and mother who work all their lives so that you can have an education and build your body, it's a blessing! When you have a wife who has been a tower of strength and shown more courage than you dreamed existed, that's the finest I know.

So I close in saying that I might have had a tough break — but I have an awful lot to live for! (from *Farewell to Yankee Fans*)

2. Talking on a Given Topic

You are required to talk about your understanding of the quote "Honesty is the best policy". Remember to use both rational and emotional appeals. You have three minutes to prepare your talk and then talk to your partner.

3. Role Play

The task involves two students, Student A and Student B. Each has a specified role as follows. Although the situation is the same, your roles are different. Learn about the role you want to play. Your preparation time is three minutes. Your conversation is limited to four minutes.

Student A: Many star athletes complain they are so closely watched by the media that their privacy has been infringed. But the entertainment media argue that it's just their job to cater to the tastes of the public and that star athletes should serve as role models. You and your partner are discussing the issue. You think it is wrong for the media to keep watching star athletes. Your partner does not agree. Try to convince him/her. Remember you should start the conversation.

Student B: Many star athletes complain they are so closely watched by the media that their privacy has been infringed. But the entertainment media argue that it's just their job to cater to the tastes of the public and that star athletes should serve as role models. You and your partner are discussing the issue. You do not think it is wrong for the media to keep watching star athletes. Your partner does not agree. Try to convince him/her. Remember your partner should start the conversation.

Notes

1. Edwin P. Whipple (1819 — 1886): American author and lecturer.
2. Quintilian (35 — 96): Roman rhetorician and critic.

Amusement Park

1. Movie to Enjoy

See the following movie and share your personal view with your classmates next week.

The Candidate (**1972**)

The movie discloses the pointlessness of American politics, especially in a race for a

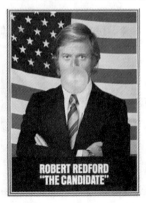

seat in the Senate. In the film, an idealistic young lawyer Bill McKay fights for the U. S. Senate, with an expectation of bringing vital issues before the voters. Once in the race, he has to face a contradiction between his ambition and his conscience.

Special Highlight

When McKay is very close in the campaign, Jarmon proposes a debate, which is supposed to provide a chance to close the last gap in the polls. Resigned to his new course of strategy, McKay agrees to give tailored answers in the debate, rather than his real opinions.

What happens to the debate then? What kind of reality in the U. S. political circle is reflected in this movie?

2. Song to Enjoy

The following is part of the lyrics to the song "Blowing in the Wind" by Bob Dylan. Find a recording of the song, listen to it and complete the lyrics.

Do you fully understand the lyrics? What is your emotional response to this song? Do you feel encouraged by it or do you feel rather down after listening to it?

> How many roads must a man walk down
> Before they call him a man?
> How many seas must a white dove sail
> Before she sleeps in the sand?
> How many times must the cannon balls fly
> Before they're forever banned?
> The answer, my friend, is blowing in the wind
> The answer is blowing in the wind
> ...

3. Community Learning

There are many differences between Chinese paintings and Western paintings in terms of emotional appeal. Please launch a 4-person team research on these differences. Then present your research findings to the class.

Unit 22

Ethos — Credibility Appeal

> I emphasize to you that we will discover ourselves through peace more than we did through confrontation and conflict.
> — Yasser Arafat[1]

Unit Goals

- To learn what ethos or credibility appeal is
- To learn the elements of credibility appeal
- To apply credibility appeal to persuasive speeches

Warm-Up

1. Do you know the meaning of "credibility"? Look this word up and think about why credibility matters much in communication.
2. If a doctor taught you English or a lawyer taught you medicine, how would you feel about the credibility of the teacher?
3. Review the samples you have learned in the previous units in this book. Do you think the speeches are credible? How does the speaker make his/her speech sound credible?

Knowledge Input

Credibility Appeal

Besides *logos* and *pathos*, *ethos* is claimed in Aristotle's *On Rhetoric* to do with speakers' moral character and credibility. As you may or may not know, the word *ethics* is derived from it. But *ethos* is actually more than that. It could be a complex of ethics, authority, charisma, image and credibility, etc. Any one who establishes the qualities of good sense, good moral character and good will will inspire *ethos* in his/her audience.

Speakers should not only exercise ascendancy over the audience, but improve the relationship with them. It is proper for someone to use the introductory part of a speech to establish his/her credibility with the audience. At the beginning of a speech, the speaker must establish his/her expertise and knowledge with the audience only by what he/she says, rather than what the audience thinks. It requires the speaker to appear competent, intelligent and honest, and interested in what is best for the audience rather than motivated by self-interest.

A speaker should be aware his/her ethic helps to establish the credibility or ethos. It is at play in a persuasive speech when the argument is being colored as ethical, or right and just. Thus, *ethos* is utilized as a rhetorical technique from either side of the coin. For example, it is usually believed to be "right" and "just" to kill murderers because they deserve to die for their wrong-doings, while it could be rhetorically argued that no one has the right to kill another person whose wrong deeds do not necessarily ever have to be repeated. Similarly, abortion could be painted with a whole palette of these ethical colors.

Ethos or credibility could be either improved or damaged by figures of speech. "Anamnesis" and "litotes" are both expected to improve *ethos*. "Anamnesis" conveys the idea by calling to memory past matters so that the speaker appears to be knowledgeable of the received wisdom from the past. "Litotes" is a means of expressing modesty or downplaying one's accomplishments in order to gain the audience's favor. However, stylistic vices or obviously artificial figures are likely to damage ethos. Throwing in foreign words to appear learned can often hurt a speaker's credibility.

In order to establish the speaker as trustworthy and credible, one has to portray as himself/herself as well-informed about the topic, confident, honest, humane and considerate, etc. These could be addressed and painted by logos (rational appeal) and pathos (emotional appeal). In the famous speech *The Gettysburg Address*, the credibility and authority of President Lincoln is depicted by these instruments of rhetoric. His ethical maxim of "all men are created equal" is both supported by the Constitution (authority) and further painted by the emotionally loaded lines as follows.

The world will little note, nor long remember what we say here, but it can never forget what they did here. It is for us the living, rather, to be dedicated here to the unfinished work that they who fought here have thus far so nobly advanced.

Knowledge Internalization

1. Pair Work

Discuss the following questions with your partner after reading the text.
1) Credibility appeal is a complex of ethics, authority, charisma, image and credibility. Could you specify what these items mean and give an example of each?
2) Choose a sample speech you learned before and discuss with your partners how the speaker establishes his/her credibility in terms of competence, intelligence and honesty.
3) Have you tried to establish your credibility when you speak publicly to others? Tell your partner how you did it.

2. Solo Work

People sometimes like songs only because they like the singers. How about you? Think about why.

3. Group Work

Divide the class into three teams. Each team is to do a research project on anamnesis, litotes or stylistic vices. Then each group chooses a spokesperson to share their findings with the class.

Lexical Power Build-Up

1. Input

Here are some useful rhetorical methods for credibility appeal.

1) *Anamnesis*

Anamnesis is the recollection of ideas known in a previons stage of existence.
- e.g. I remember Arlene Howard, who gave me her fallen son's police shield as a reminder of all that was lost. And I still carry his badge.

  Was it not Socrates who said the unexamined life is not worth living?

  No one has been a more consistent opponent of Communism than I have for the last twenty-five years. I will unsay no words that I've spoken about it.

2) *Litotes*

Litotes is a figure of speech consisting of an understatement, where the speaker uses a negative of a word to mean the opposite.
- e.g. We made a difference. We made the city stronger, we made the city freer, and we left her in good hands. All in all, not bad, not bad at all.

  I do not mistrust the future.

No other definite line can be drawn between the inestimable liberty of the press and its demoralizing licentiousness.

2. Pair Work

Discuss with your partner why the use of anamnesis or litotes helps build up your credibility. Use the examples listed above to support your ideas.

3. Group Work

Each group should choose an advertisement done by a celebrity. Analyze what the celebrity says in the advertisement and tell whether he/she is using anamnesis or litotes. Comment on the use of such rhetoric and then present your opinions to the class.

4. Solo Work

Think about yourself giving a speech to your fellow students. Which do you think would help you more, anamnesis or litotes? Why?

Comprehensive Input

Below is the former Secretary of Education Dr. William J. Bennett[2]'s lecture at Hillsdale College in 2002.

Teaching the Virtues (Excerpt)

"Teaching the virtues" seemed very much to me then — and still seems to me today — a concern of prime importance for the American people. And I think the answer regarding how to teach the virtues is pretty straightforward.

Aristotle had a good read on it, and modern psychology and other contemporary studies back him up: We teach by habit, we teach by precept, and we teach by example.

Aristotle says that habituation at an early age makes more than a little difference; it can make almost all the difference. So if you want kids to learn what work is, you should have them work. If you want them to learn what responsibility means, you should hold them responsible. If you want them to learn what perseverance is, you should encourage them to persevere. And you should start as early as possible. Of course, this is harder to do than to say. Being a parent and teaching these things is a very rigorous exercise.

Precepts are also important. The Ten Commandments, the principles of American democracy, rules of courteous behavior — these and other lists of rights and wrongs should be provided to young people. But as we provide them, young people need to know that we take these precepts seriously.

That leads to the third part of teaching virtue that Aristotle talked about, which is example. And that, probably, is the one we should emphasize the most. I have been to school after school where the administration thinks it can solve its "values problem" by teaching a course in values. I do not believe in courses in values. I do not think that's the way to go about solving the problem.

If we want young people to take right and wrong seriously, there is an indispensable condition: They must be in the presence of adults who take right and wrong seriously. Only in this way will they see that virtue is not just a game, not just talk, but rather that it is something that grown-up people, people who have responsibilities in the world and at home, take seriously…. Our children won't take honesty seriously until we grown-ups demand honesty of ourselves and others, including our leaders. Needless to say, the Clinton years were not good years for impressing the virtue of honesty on our kids.

Comprehensive Practice

1. Pair Work

Tell your partner how you feel about the speech's morality and credibility. Find out how the speaker establishes the qualities of good sense, good moral character and good will.

2. Pair Work

Work with your partner and point out the use of anamnesis and litotes in the speech. What is the effect of such rhetorical devices?

3. Solo Work

Compose a short persuasive speech based on one of the following topics. Remember: you need to have a central point and you need to use the three appeals properly.

1) Being a volunteer worker
2) From zero to hero
3) All doors open to courtesy.
4) Working for excellence or working for satisfaction?

4. Group Work

Give a presentation to your group members about something you are good at, such as paper-cutting, embroidery, swimming, or musical instrument playing. Feel how your competence and confidence may help you build up your credibility.

5. Class Work

Deliver the speech you have composed to your class. The class should comment on the speaker's use of appeals and give him/her suggestions. Based on the persuasiveness of the speakers, choose the three most effective speeches in your class.

Teachers may record students' performance and let them watch afterwards and ask the speakers to evaluate their own performance.

Extra Input

The following is an excerpt of Bill Gates' 2005 speech "Unleashing your creativity". As one of the most successful entrepreneurs in the world, Bill Gates delivered this speech to encourage the audience's natural inventiveness, creativity and willingness to solve tough problems.

Unleashing Your Creativity

I've always been an optimist and I suppose that is rooted in my belief that the power of creativity and intelligence can make the world a better place.

...

When my friend Paul Allen and I started Microsoft 30 years ago, we had a vision of "a computer on every desk and in every home", which probably sounded a little too optimistic at a time when most computers were the size of refrigerators. But we believed that personal computers would change the world. And they have.

...

But for all the cool things that a person can do with a PC, there are lots of other ways we can put our creativity and intelligence to work to improve our world. There are still far too many people in the world whose most basic needs go unmet. Every year, for example, millions of people die from diseases that are easy to prevent or treat in the developed world.

I believe that my own good fortune brings with it a responsibility to give back to the world. My wife, Melinda, and I have committed to improving health and education in a way that can help as many people as possible.

As a father, I believe that the death of a child in Africa is no less poignant or tragic than the death of a child anywhere else. And that it doesn't take much to make an immense difference in these children's lives.... I'm excited by the possibilities I see for medicine, for education and, of course, for technology. And I believe that through our natural inventiveness, creativity and willingness to solve tough problems, we're going to make some amazing achievements in all these areas in my lifetime.

New Hurdles

1. Retelling

Listen to the passage and retell it immediately after you have heard it.

Brian Gutrick traveled 1 200 miles and paid $ 12 000 for a fresh start.

The newly married construction worker wanted a job with better prospects and more stability, so he took out a student loan and headed from Virginia to a trade school in Alabama to study heating, ventilation and air conditioning.

Brian finished the program in 2007 at the top of his class, but he landed in an economy already beginning to teeter. Before he could find a foothold, the country had slid into the worst recession since the Great Depression of the 1930s.

"I've been beating doors down. I've sent out at least five hundred resumes and just no answer," says the 32-year-old, who has still not found a job. "I have three kids and a wife. I have to do something."

He is persistent. He wears a suit and tie to interviews — "just for a construction job, some people go in dirty boots and everything!" — and takes proof of his grades and accreditation. But he is getting nowhere and he is not alone. Since he left trade school, 7.2 million Americans have lost their jobs, bringing the total number of unemployed to 14.7 million. The unemployment rate now stands at 9.5 percent and will almost certainly hit double digits before the year is out.

This blow to the labor market in the world's biggest economy caught many unawares. In 2007 the U.S. had one of the lowest unemployment rates in the Organization for Economic Co-operation and Development, but now it has one of the highest, beaten only by Spain, Ireland, Hungary and Slovakia.

People who have lost their jobs are losing their health insurance and their homes. The number relying on government food stamps has risen by 6.2 million since the recession started, and they now feed a near-record one in nine Americans.

2. Talking on a Given Topic

You are required to talk about your experience of globalization using the topic "Globalization and I". Remember to use your own experience as examples. You have three minutes to prepare your talk and then talk to your partner.

3. Role Play

The task involves two students, Student A and Student B. Each has a specified role as follows. Although the situation is the same, your roles are different. Learn about the role you want to play. Your preparation time is three minutes. Your conversation is limited to four minutes.

Student A: Many college students are complaining about their tight schedule. They do not have spare time to do what they are interested in. College life seems quite different from what they imagined. You and your partner are discussing the topic. You think college students should devote all their time and energy to academic life. Your partner does not agree. Try to convince him/her. Remember you should start the conversation.

Student B: Many college students are complaining about their tight schedule. They do not have spare time to do what they are interested in. College life seems quite different from what they imagined. You and your partner are discussing the topic. You do not think college students should devote all their time and energy to academic life. Your partner does not agree. Try to convince him/her. Remember your partner should start the conversation.

Notes

1. Yasser Arafat (1929 — 2004): Palestinian leader, Chairman of the Palestine Liberation Organization (PLO), President of the Palestinian National Authority and leader of the Fatah political party.
2. William J. Bennett: He was chosen by President Reagan to head the National Endowment for the Humanities in 1981 and was named Secretary of Education in 1985. In 1989, President Bush appointed him director of the Office of National Drug Control Policy. The special identities have made all his books and speeches convincing and impressive.

Amusement Park

1. Movie to Enjoy

See the following movie and share your personal view with your classmates next week.

Mr. Smith Goes to Washington (**1939**)

Mr. Smith Goes to Washington is a comedy film reflecting many of the shortcomings

of the political process through one man's effect on American politics. Although it was controversial when it was released, it was actually successful at the box office. Alben W. Barkley, the Senate Majority Leader, called the film "silly and stupid", and said it "makes the Senate look like a bunch of crooks." However, the Library of Congress added the film to the United States National Film Registry in 1989, for being "culturally, historically, or aesthetically significant".

Special Highlight

An interesting part of the film is when Paine accuses Smith of profiting from his bill by producing false evidence that Smith owned the land in question. Watch this part carefully and make sure you understand what is happening.

What is Smith's response after learning of Paine's betrayal? What does the story tell you about politics and politicians?

2. Song to Enjoy

The following is part of the lyrics to the song "Never Had a Dream Come True" by S Club 7. Find a recording of the song, listen to it and complete the lyrics.

I never had a dream come true
Till the day I found you.
Even though I pretend that I moved on,
You'll always be my baby.
I never found the words to say,
You're the one I think about each day.
And I know no matter where life takes me to,
A part of me will always be with you.
Somewhere in my memory, I lost all sense of time.
And tomorrow can never be
Cause yesterday is all that fills my mind.

There's no use lookin' back or wonderin',
How it could be now or might have been.
Oh, this I know, but still I can not find ways to let you go…

3. Community Learning

The whole class is divided into several groups, each of which acts as the public relations department for a company. Since the greatest credibility of all comes from word-of-mouth, you should make a strategy for the establishment of the credibility of your company utilizing favorable word-of-mouth. The audience will judge each group's plan and ask each speaker relevant questions to test its feasibility.

You may record each other's performance and then evaluate your own performance.

Unit 23

Persuasive Speeches on Questions of Value

> As we become ever more diverse, we must work harder to unite around our common values and our common humanity.
> — Bill Clinton

Unit Goals

- To understand what speeches on questions of value are
- To learn to analyze questions of value
- To learn to organize speeches on questions of value
- To compose and deliver a speech on a question of value

Warm-Up

1. Is it always easy to tell right from wrong? Why or why not?
2. What are your principles when trying to make judgments concerning what is right or wrong, good or bad?
3. Do you think the values of the various peoples in the world are generally shared or are they very dissimilar and can not be harmonized?

Knowledge Input

Persuasive Speeches to Convince

When you give a persuasive speech on a question of value, you are basically talking about "Is it good or is it bad? Moral or immoral? Just or unjust?" You are making fundamental value judgments concerning what is right or wrong. Your task is to convince the audience of what you think is right and seek intellectual agreement from them. A successful persuasive speech on questions of value can often influence or even change an audience's opinion about significant issues. However, you are not asking listeners to do anything.

You may have already realized that questions of value are a lot more than matters of personal preferences or personal opinions. You can not make and support a claim on a question of value simply because you like it or you think it's cool. What you need to do is justify your statement — to state the facts, statistics and reasons that will back up your claim.

In planning a persuasive speech on a question of value, the following steps are essential.

First, it is essential to understand the topic. Some fundamental value questions, such as human cloning, race relations, and violence on TV are very complicated issues and you need to make sure you know what they are about before you can talk intelligently and responsibly about them.

Then, it is essential to take a definite stand and stay committed to it. A definite stand does not mean an absolute point. An effective persuasion should make a definite point, and urge the listeners to adopt a certain position or belief. In this sense, an either-or point is much more valued than a both-and point. Yet Chinese students are quite often afraid of committing themselves to a clear-cut point. They try to "stay in the middle" to avoid a strong, clear point. This is not a good habit. Being ambiguous and vague is no way of avoiding being absolute; it will instead damage your credibility.

Also, you need to decide on your position statement. Your position statement states your central idea, which is to be supported with related points and materials. A statement of value indicates that you will present arguments, facts and evidence to persuade the audience that something is good, just, wise, and so on. Your position statement covers the controlling idea of the whole speech, yet it should also be specific enough to state your exact opinion. You can find some samples of position statements in Lexical Power Build-Up.

Knowing your purpose and point is not enough, you still need to do research work to find and select the best supporting materials. Your supporting materials and evidence may include expert opinion, statistics, factual instances, personal experiences, and so on. In order to obtain a variety of apt, effective evidence, doing research is a must.

Now comes the task of organizing your speech and working out your major supporting points. You can prepare an outline of main points and needed information and evidence. A sample is given below.

Speech Outline

Topic: Human cloning

Purpose: To persuade the audience that human cloning is ethically unsound and technically risky

Central idea (position statement):

Due to the inefficiency and uncertainty of animal cloning and the lack of understanding about reproductive cloning, it would be highly unethical and risky to attempt to clone humans at this point of time.

Main points:

1. *The success rate of animal cloning is only about 1 or 2 viable offspring for every 100 experiments.*
2. *About 30% of clones born alive are affected with "large-offspring syndrome".*
3. *There are still many unknowns concerning reproductive cloning.*
4. *Scientists do not know how cloning could impact mental development.*

Once you have all the points and evidence in place, you can go on to compose and then rehearse the speech. While composing the speech, do not forget to use the three appeals, and do not forget to design a forceful beginning and ending for your speech. In delivery, try to establish your credibility and trustworthiness through controlling your vocal quality and maintaining eye contact.

Knowledge Internalization

1. Pair Work

Discuss the following questions with your partner after reading the text.

1) Why is it often necessary to do research work when you are preparing a speech to convince?
2) Discuss the pros and cons of "staying in the middle" when choosing a stand. What are you inclined to do, take a definite stand or avoid taking it?

2. Solo Work

Choose one of the following topics and try to decide on your stand. Then do research work to find material to support your stand. Choose the one you know more about or the one you feel strongly about.

1) IQ tests and intelligence
2) Unlicensed software
3) Space program funding
4) Sex education in school
5) Women leaders mean a more peaceful world

Lexical Power Build-Up

1. Input

Here are some samples of position statements for persuasive speeches on questions of value.

Topic — Internet forums: *Internet forums are not as effective as believed as an indicator of public opinion.*

Topic — Movie industry: *Given the present situation in the entertainment market, big-budget movies represent the best future for the Chinese movie industry.*

Topic — Leadership: *As far as leadership is concerned, people management skills are far more important than specialist knowledge.*

Topic — Medical experiment with animals: *Even though these procedures are for medical development, it is at the animal's expense and dismisses animal welfare altogether.*

Topic — Sexual harassment: *Nine times out of ten, sexual harassment is not about sex; it is about power — the abuse of power can lead to sexual harassment.*

Topic — Office romance: *Although people spend more time at work than almost anywhere else, the dangers and risks of office romance are quite high too.*

2. Qualifying Your Statement

If you qualify your statement, you add some information, evidence, or phrase in order to make it less absolute or less generalized.

Here are some ways to qualify your statement.

1) Use "frequency" qualifiers such as *most, almost, usually, practically, in effect, hardly ever, for the most part, to all intents and purposes, to a great extent, up to a point, more or less*, etc.

 e.g. *Up to a point* we can agree with Blair when he argues that nationalization is not an effective way to organize industry.

2) Use "speculative" qualifiers such as *may, might, probably, seemingly, apparently, presumably*, etc.

 e.g. The UN Security Council is *probably* the most powerful agent of peace in today's world.

3) Add a qualifying phrase or subordinate clause to your statement.

 e.g. *Despite* this month's unemployment figures, we can be *more or less* certain that the economic downturn has completed its cycle.

3. Solo Work

Qualify the following statements to make them less absolute or less general.

1) President Bush never says anything intelligent.
2) Any man who gives all his salary to his wife is a fool.
3) Contributing to the Mutual Fund is the best investment you could make.
4) Top students will always turn out to be top employees because of their outstanding qualities.

4. Group Work

What other "qualifiers" can you use to qualify your statement? Please make a list of more qualifiers and share them with your classmates.

5. Solo Work

Reconstruct a position statement based on the topic and stand you have chosen in Knowledge Internalization.

6. Solo Work

Sometimes it is not what you say, but the way you say it that matters. So rehearse stating your position statement. Pay special attention to your volume, speed and stress. Make sure your point will be clearly, effortlessly understood.

Comprehensive Input

Below is the excerpt of the TV speech made by Albert Einstein on February 12, 1950. He spoke about his conviction of the wrongfulness of national armament.

Peace in the Atomic Age (Excerpt)

I am grateful to you for the opportunity to express my conviction in this most important political question.

The idea of achieving security through national armament is, at the present state of military technique, a disastrous illusion. On the part of the United States, this illusion has been particularly fostered by the fact that this country succeeded first in producing an atomic bomb. The belief seemed to prevail that in the end it were possible to achieve decisive military superiority.

In this way, any potential opponent would be intimidated, and security, so ardently desired by all of us, brought to us, and to all of humanity. The maxim which we have been following during these last five years has been, in short: security through superior military power, whatever the cost.

The armament race between the U. S. A and the U. S. S. R. , originally supposed to be a preventive measure, assumes hysterical character. On both sides, the means to mass destruction are perfected with feverish haste — behind the respective walls of secrecy. The H-bomb appears on the public horizon as a probably attainable goal.

If successful, radioactive poisoning of the atmosphere and hence annihilation of any life on earth has been brought within the range of technical possibilities. The ghostlike character of this development lies in its apparently compulsory trend. Every step appears as the unavoidable consequence of the preceding one. In the end, there beckons more and more clearly general annihilation.

... It is impossible to achieve peace as long as every single action is taken with a possible future conflict in view. The leading point of view of all political actions should therefore be: What can we do to bring about a peaceful co-existence and even loyal co-operation of the nations?

The first problem is to do away with mutual fear and distrust. Solemn renunciation of violence (not only with respect to means of mass destruction) is undoubtedly necessary.

... In the last analysis, every kind of peaceful co-operation among men is primarily based on mutual trust and only secondly on institutions such as courts of justice and police. This holds for nations as well as for individuals. And the basis of trust is loyal to give and take.

Comprehensive Practice

1. Pair Work

Discuss the following questions with your partner.
1) What is the purpose of this speech?
2) Which sentence expresses the central idea of this speech? How is it qualified?
3) On what different levels does the speech support the central idea? Are these levels clearly presented?

2. Solo Work

Compose a speech using the topic and the position statement you have worked on. Use the materials you have found in your research work. Make sure your speech has clear organization and all the details are presented logically and effectively.

3. Class Work

Practice delivering your speech and then deliver your speech in your group and listen to your group members' comments. Then each group selects its best speaker to deliver the speech to the whole class. Listen to the speeches and give feedback to each speaker. Your feedback should cover both the content and delivery. Then choose the best speaker of the day.

Extra Input

The following are two excerpts of sample speeches on questions of value. Study the excerpts carefully and find out what facts and value judgments are included. Do you think the judgment is fairly and effectively made?

Using the Talent You Have (Beginning)

One of the interesting things I have discovered in my 45 years as a teacher and school principal is that everyone is good at something.

Some people are good at particular school subjects; some are good at sport; some make great actors or excellent speakers. Some people know how to get on with others; some have a great sense of humor; some are good at making things; some are good listeners; some make good friends.

Every single person has something worthwhile to contribute and it is very important that you never let others "put you down". There are hundreds of examples of people in the world who have believed what others have said about them, and failed; there are just as many who have refused to be influenced by the opinions of others, and been successful.

The brilliant scientist and inventor, Thomas Edison, is a good example of this.

He was thrown out of school when he was 12 because he was thought to be dumb. He was terrible at mathematics, unable to focus, and had difficulty with words and speech. However, he refused to allow the things said by his teachers to stop him from doing what he wanted to do.

And he was an extremely hard worker, sometimes working twenty hours a day. His hard work was rewarded as he patented 1 093 inventions in his life time, the largest number on record.

Another famous achiever, who refused to be discouraged by failure, is night show host, Jay Leno. Leno is mildly dyslexic, and he did not do very well in school. However, he…was determined not to give up, despite the fact that others thought he did not have enough talent. …

The Morality of Birth Control (Excerpt)
Margaret Sanger (November 18, 1921)

…The one issue upon which there seems to be most uncertainty and disagreement exists in the moral side of the subject of birth control. …Letters were sent to the most eminent men and women in the world. We asked in this letter the following questions.

1) Is over-population a menace to the peace of the world?
2) Would the dissemination of... scientific birth control information...be the logical method of checking the problem of over-population?
3) Would knowledge of birth control change the moral attitude of men and women toward the marriage bond or lower the moral standards of the youth of the country?
4) Do you believe that knowledge which enables parents to limit the families will make for human happiness, and raise the moral, social and intellectual standards of population?

...We know that every advance that woman has made in the last half century has been made with opposition, all of which has been based upon the grounds of immorality. When women fought for higher education, it was said that this would cause her to become immoral and she would lose her place in... the home. When women asked for the right to vote, it was said that this would lower her standard of morals, that it was not fit for she should meet with and mix with the members of the opposite sex, but we notice that there was no objection to her meeting with the same members of the opposite sex when she went to church.

The church has ever opposed the progress of woman on the ground that her freedom would lead to immorality. We ask the church to have more confidence in women...We stand on the principle that Birth Control should be available to every adult man and woman...We claim that woman should have the right over her own body and to say if she shall or shall not be a mother, as she sees fit...

New Hurdles

1. Retelling

Listen to the passage and retell it immediately after you have heard it.

The Father-and-Son Team

Born in 1962, Rick Hoyt suffered from brain damage. He was left with the inability to move his limbs and was unable to speak. When Rick was 11, his father Dick took him to Tufts University and asked if anything could be done to help his son communicate. The engineers firmly said no because there was no activity in his son's brain. But Dick requested that they tell his son a joke and when they did, Rick laughed. This convinced the engineers to create a special computer which Rick could control to communicate with people.

During Rick's high school years, a classmate became paralyzed from a car accident.

The school organized a five-mile benefit run for the student. Rick said to his father, "Dad, I want to do that!"

His father took on the challenge and pushed his son in a wheelchair for five miles. They finished next to last. That night Rick said to his father, "When we were running, it felt like I wasn't disabled anymore!"

These words forever changed Dick and set him on a life-long mission of giving his son that feeling of not being disabled. "Team Hoyt" began.

Their first goal was to run in the 1979 Boston Marathon, but they met with too much resistance from race officials. But they persevered. When the father and son team finished in the top quarter in the 1981 Boston Marathon, attitudes toward them began to change.

From 1979 to 2008, the father and son team have participated in a total of 958 sporting events. Their best time in a marathon was 2 hours and 40 minutes, just 35 minutes from the world record! What a remarkable feat!

If Dick and Rick could give any words of wisdom, it would be to "Yes, you can." "Cannot" is not a word in the Team Hoyt vocabulary.

2. Talking on a Given Topic

You are required to talk about a principle or belief that you hold as the backbone of your value system. Tell clearly what this principle or belief is, why it is so important to you, and how it has helped or guided you so far. You have three minutes to prepare your talk and then give it to your partner.

3. Role Play

The task involves two students, Student A and Student B. Each has a specified role as follows. Although the situation is the same, your roles are different. Learn about the role you want to play. Your preparation time is three minutes. Your conversation is limited to four minutes.

Student A: You are a reporter for the student union newsletter. You are interviewing a student in your university who started his/her campus business and became successful. You ask him/her how he/she is doing with the business and you want to know what values or principles are underlying his/her success. Remember you should start the conversation.

Student B: You are a student who started your retail business on campus and became successful. Tell the reporter what your business is like, what the business has brought to you and share with him/her the motivation behind the success story. Bring the conversation to a positive, fruitful ending.

Amusement Park

1. Movie to Enjoy

See the following movie and share your personal view with your classmates next week.

Tootsie (**1982**)

Michael Dorsey (Dustin Hoffman) is an actor approaching 40. Although as an actor he is very professional, he is a perfectionist. Nobody in New York wants to hire him anymore because he is so difficult to work with, or he is either too old or too young for a role. Not having worked in four months, he eventually hears of an opening on the soap opera "Southwest General". In desperation, he shaves himself clean, cross-dresses as a woman, auditions as "Dorothy Michaels" and eventually gets the part…

Special Highlight

When the cast is forced to perform a scene live, Michael improvises a speech and reveals that he is actually the character's twin brother who took her place to avenge her. It is a hilarious speech to hear and see, with Dustin Hoffman caught right between being a man and woman at the same time.

What truths has Michael Dorsey found out about the other sex with the advantage of being a "woman"? Would he ever know so much about woman if he did not cross-dress?

2. Song to Enjoy

The following is part of the lyrics to the song "The Sound of Silence" by Paul Simon. Find a recording of the song, listen to it and complete the lyrics.

Compared with the R & B style, this song is believed to be unique in some ways. What special qualities do you think this song has?

>Hello darkness, my old friend,
>I've come to talk with you again,
>Because a vision softly creeping,
>Left its seeds while I was sleeping,
>And the vision that was planted in my brain
>Still remains within the sound of silence.
>In restless dreams I walked alone,
>Narrow streets of cobblestone,
>'Neath the halo of a street lamp,
>I turned my collar to the cold and damp
>When my eyes were stabbed by the flash of a neon light

That split the night
And touched the sound of silence...

3. Community Learning

In your dormitory, talk about the quotation that has influenced you most. Tell your friends what the quote is, what truth it reveals, and how it has had an impact on your life or on your understanding of life. Share with each other the wisdom and personal experiences, and make the quotations a collection. You may write the quotes on paper and put it on the wall.

Unit 24

Rhetoric for Public Policy Speeches

> A conservative is a man with two perfectly good legs who, however, has never learned how to walk forward.
> — Franklin D. Roosevelt[1]

Unit Goals

- To know what public policy speech is
- To learn how to improve public policy speeches through rhetoric
- To understand the rhetorical devices used by politicians and their speechwriters
- To learn how to establish charisma and greatness through public policy speeches

Warm-Up

1. Have you ever put forward any suggestion or proposal to improve the management of your school or your class? What was your policy and how did you put it forward?
2. If you are running for chair of the student union, how would you deliver an address of blueprint of your policies?
3. There are many presidential inaugural addresses in the U. S. , most of which seem to be very persuasive to the public. Who do you think is the most persuasive president in the U. S. ? What are your reasons?

Knowledge Input

Public Policy Speeches

A policy is a program or a sequence of actions adopted by social groups, governments,

political parties or business organizations. A policy influences, guides and determines decisions and actions. A speech on public policy is about whether or not a specific course of action should be taken. For example, a speech to persuade the audience that factories causing serious air or water pollution should be closed down is a speech on public policy.

In a public policy speech, the speaker can have two purposes: to gain the agreement of the audience and further, or to gain immediate action on the part of the audience. That is to say, the speaker must convince the audience of the merits of his/her ideas and then move the audience to action in support of the policy.

The three basic issues to be covered in a speech on public policy include: the need for a policy, the policy itself and the feasibility of the policy.

There is no point in arguing for a policy unless you can show a need for it. So your first step is to identity a problem calling for a new policy. The second basic issue of policy speeches is to explain the policy or the plan you are proposing. Once you have shown that a problem exists, you must explain your plan for solving it. This part deals with the issues of "what to do" and "how to do" to solve the existing problem. The third basic issue of policy speeches is feasibility or practicality of the policy. Once you have presented a plan, you must show that it will work without creating new and more serious problems.

In addition, effective organization is crucial when you seek to persuade listeners on a question of policy. Two organization schemes are especially useful for policy speeches: the Problem-Cause-Solution Order and the Monroe's Motivated Sequence.

Problem-Cause-Solution Order Your speech will be developed in three main parts. In the first main part, you demonstrate the problem and the need for a new policy. In the second main part, you analyze the causes of such problem. And then you explain your plan for solving the problem, showing your plan is practical and effective because it targets the causes. Following this order, a sample speech outline is given as follows.

Specific Purpose: *To persuade my audience that colleges and universities should take stronger action to control campus crime.*

Part I (*problem*): *Violent crime on college campuses is a serious problem that needs to be addressed right away.*

Part Ⅱ (cause): *There are three major causes specific to college life for the growth of campus crime.*

Part Ⅱ (solution): *An effective solution must deal with all three major causes of the problem.*

The Monroe's Motivated Sequence   In this organization pattern, the speech is divided into five parts:

1) Attention: Gain the attention of the audience.
2) Need: Make the audience feel the need for change.
3) Satisfaction: Satisfy the sense of need by providing a solution to the problem.
4) Visualization: Intensify desire for the solution by visualizing its benefits.
5) Action: Urge the audience to take action in support of the solution.

The Problem-Cause-Solution Order and the Monroe's Motivated Sequence have proved to be clear and effective on countless policy issues. Try it out and you will find it can work for your speech, too.

Knowledge Internalization

1. Pair Work

Discuss the following questions with your partner after reading the text.

1) What is the difference between speeches of value and speeches of policy?
2) How would you decide how much of your speech is devoted to need, policy and feasibility?
3) In a speech of pubic policy, how should you use the three appeals?

2. Solo Work

Develop a speech outline with either the Problem-Cause-Solution Order or/and the Monroe's Motivated Sequence, using one of the topics below.

1) Teenage smoking
2) Drunk driving
3) Identity theft crimes
4) Sexually-explicit media content

Lexical Power Build-Up

1. Lexical Input

Here are some useful rhetorical devices for public policy speeches:

1) Anaphora

Anaphora is a deliberate repetition of a word or phrase at the beginning of several successive verses, clauses, or paragraphs.

e. g. Today, *our* fellow citizens, *our* way of life, *our* very freedom came under attack in a series of deliberate and deadly terrorist attacks.

We shall not flag or fail. *We shall* go on to the end. *We shall* fight in France, *we shall* fight on the seas and oceans, *we shall*...

We will not tire, *we will not* falter, and *we will not* fail.

I will not yield; *I will not* rest; *I will not* relent.

Never tiring, *never* yielding, *never* finishing,...

2) Antithesis

Antithesis is the juxtaposition of contrasting ideas in a balanced structure.

e. g. We must learn to live together as brothers or perish together as fools.

The more acute the experience, the less articulate its expression.

If a free society cannot help the many who are poor, it cannot save the few who are rich.

3) Imagery Words

dream (idea), sweat (toil), hand (help), heart (commitment), fire (enthusiasm), cold (winter), heat (summer), fall (die), etc.

2. Group Work

The words frequently used by either Democrats or Republicans in the U. S. are as follows. Conduct a team research project and collect the possible imagery words and their related conceptual counterparts for the keywords in balloons.

Then share your findings with other groups in your class.

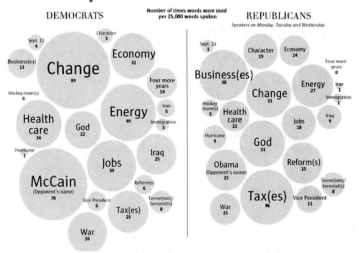

3. Solo Work

Work on your previous speech drafts and see if you can reconstruct some of your sentences using the rhetorical devices you have learned.

Comprehensive Input

Below is Franklin Delano Roosevelt's first inaugural address in March 1933. By late winter 1933, the U. S. had already endured more than three years of economic depression. Roosevelt aimed to declare war on the Great Depression.

Franklin D. Roosevelt: First Inaugural Address (Excerpt)

This is preeminently the time to speak the truth, the whole truth, frankly and boldly. Nor need we shrink from honestly facing conditions in our country today. This great nation will endure as it has endured, will revive and will prosper.

So, first of all, let me assert my firm belief that the only thing we have to fear is fear itself — nameless, unreasoning, unjustified terror which paralyzes needed efforts to convert retreat into advance. In every dark hour of our national life, a leadership of frankness and vigor has met with that understanding and support of the people themselves which is essential to victory. And I am convinced that you will again give that support to leadership in these critical days.

In such a spirit on my part and on yours we face our common difficulties. They concern, thank God, only material things. Values have shrunk to fantastic levels; taxes have risen; our ability to pay has fallen; government of all kinds is faced by serious curtailment of income; the means of exchange are frozen in the currents of trade; the withered leaves of industrial enterprise lie on every side; farmers find no markets for their produce; and the savings of many years in thousands of families are gone. More important, a host of unemployed citizens face the grim problem of existence and an equally great number toil with little return. Only a foolish optimist can deny the dark realities of the moment.

And yet our distress comes from no failure of substance. We are stricken by no plague of locusts. Compared with the perils which our forefathers conquered, because they believed and were not afraid, we have still much to be thankful for. Nature still offers her bounty and human efforts have multiplied it. Plenty is at our doorstep, but a generous use of it languishes in the very sight of the supply...

Comprehensive Practice

1. Solo Work

Read the speech aloud to yourself. Do you think you can effectively control your voice so that you sound determined and powerful?

2. Pair Work

Discuss with your partner the use of the three appeals in this speech. Are the appeals properly and sufficiently used?

3. Group Work

Analyze the organization and the use of rhetorical devices in this speech. Share your findings with other groups in your class.

4. Solo Work

Compose a short speech based on the speech outline you have finished. Use the three appeals and other rhetorical devices as you see fit.

5. Class Work

Deliver the speech you have written to your class. The listeners can ask questions concerning the policy proposed in the speech.

6. Class Work

Running for Monitor

Select four candidates in your class to run for monitor. Organize a public debate where the candidates can make clear their policies and find fault with others' policies. The class will then judge which candidate is the winner.

7. Group Work

Form four-person groups where three members are to play the role of speechwriters and the other is to be the presenter. Design, compose and deliver a policy speech. The audience will judge each team's composition and presentation to see which speech is best written and which is best delivered.

Extra Input

The following is part of Winston Churchill's speech in Harrow School — *Never Give In*. This speech is delivered on October 29, 1941 and it has become one of Churchill's most quoted speeches.

Almost a year has passed since I came down here at your Head Master's kind invitation in order to cheer myself and cheer the hearts of a few of my friends by singing some of our own songs.

The ten months that have passed have seen very terrible catastrophic events in the world — ups and downs, misfortunes — but can anyone sitting here this afternoon, this

October afternoon, not feel deeply thankful for what has happened in the time that has passed and for the very great improvement in the position of our country and of our home?

Why, when I was here last time we were quite alone, desperately alone, and we had been so for five or six months. We were poorly armed. We are not so poorly armed today; but then we were very poorly armed. We had the unmeasured menace of the enemy and their air attack still beating upon us, and you yourselves had had experience of this attack; and I expect you are beginning to feel impatient that there has been this long lull with nothing particular turning up!

But we must learn to be equally good at what is short and sharp and what is long and tough. It is generally said that the British are often better at the last. They do not expect to move from crisis to crisis; they do not always expect that each day will bring up some noble chance of war; but when they very slowly make up their minds that the thing has to be done and the job put through and finished, then, even if it takes months — if it takes years — they do it.

Another lesson I think we may take, just throwing our minds back to our meeting here ten months ago and now, is that appearances are often very deceptive, and as Kipling well says, we must "...meet with Triumph and Disaster. And treat those two impostors just the same".

You cannot tell from appearances how things will go. Sometimes imagination makes things out far worse than they are; yet without imagination not much can be done. Those people who are imaginative see many more dangers than perhaps exist; certainly many more than will happen; but then they must also pray to be given that extra courage to carry this far-reaching imagination.

But for everyone, surely, what we have gone through in this period — I am addressing myself to the School — surely from this period of ten months, this is the lesson:

Never give in. Never give in. Never, never, never, never — in nothing, great or small, large or petty — never give in, except to convictions of honor and good sense. Never yield to force. Never yield to the apparently overwhelming might of the enemy...

New Hurdles

1. Retelling

Listen to the passage and retell it immediately after you have heard it.

If a five-year-old child came to ask you what a credit crunch is, how could you explain this? Below is a fairy tale making the credit crunch suitable for children. Can you tell us the reality after reading it?

Once upon a time, there was a blameless girl called Consumerella who did not have enough money to buy all the lovely things she wanted. So she went to her Fairy Godmother, who called a man called Rumpelstiltskin who lived on Wall Street and claimed to be able to spin straw into gold. Rumpelstiltskin sent the Fairy Godmother the recipe for this magic spell. It was in tiny, tiny writing, so she did not read it but hoped the Sorcerers' Exchange Commission had checked it.

The Fairy Godmother carried away straw derivative at a bargain price and lent Consumerella 125% of the money she needed. Consumerella bought a gown, a palace and a Mercedes — and spent the rest on champagne. The first repayment was due at midnight, which Consumerella missed. (The result of overindulgence, although some blamed the pronouncements of the Toastmaster, a man called Peston.) Consumerella's credit rating turned into a pumpkin and the spell was broken: the vaults were not full of gold, but straw.

All seemed lost until Santa Claus and his helpers, men with fairytale names such as Darling and Bernanke, began handing out presents. In January, Consumerella's credit card statement arrived and she discovered that Santa Claus had paid for the gifts by taking out a loan in her name. They all lived miserably ever after.

2. Talking on a Given Topic

You are required to put forward a proposal to solve the problem of students' cheating in exams. Try to persuade your partner to accept it. You have three minutes to prepare your talk and then give it to your partner.

3. Role Play

The task involves two students, Student A and Student B. Each has a specified role as follows. Although the situation is the same, your roles are different. Learn about the role you want to play. Your preparation time is three minutes. Your conversation is limited to four minutes.

Student A: You are the CEO of a company. You do not think bonus could be used as gifts to reward your employees, while many other employers always choose to do so. Your employee disagrees with you. Try to convince him/her. Remember you should start the conversation.

Student B: You are one of the employees in the company. You think bonus could be used as gifts to reward those performing well since other employers always choose to do so. Your employer disagrees with you. Try to convince him/her. Remember your boss should start the conversation.

Notes

1. Franklin Roosevelt (1882 – 1945): the only U. S. President elected to more than two terms. He won his first of four presidential elections in 1932. He led the United States through the Great Depression and most of World War II. Roosevelt is ranked by historians as one of the most successful of U. S. Presidents.

Amusement Park

1. Movie to Enjoy

See the following movie and share your personal view with your classmates next week.

Fahrenheit 9/11 (2004)

Taking a critical look at the presidency of George W. Bush, the War on Terrorism and its coverage in the American news media, *Fahrenheit 9/11* was awarded the Golden Palm and held the record for highest box office receipts by a general release political film. It generated substantial controversy and criticism after its release less than four months before the 2004 U. S. presidential election. While *Fahrenheit 9/11* was thought by some experts to contain distortions and untruths, there has been speculation about the making of a sequel to be called *Fahrenheit 9/11 1/2*, the plot of which was expected to pick up where the first one left off.

Special Highlight

Turning to the Iraq war, the documentary compares the lives of the Iraqis before and after the invasion. It shows that Iraqis enjoyed relatively happy lives until the U. S. military invasion. Pains have been taken to collect some convincing quotes from news organizations and embedded journalists, so as to show the war cheerleading in the U. S. media and general bias of

journalists.

Do you think the director is right in suggesting that the Iraqi war was based on a lie? What do you think about the nature of all wars?

2. Song to Enjoy

The following is part of the lyrics to the song "Strange Fruit" by Billie Holiday. Find a recording of the song, listen to it and complete the lyrics.

What is the "strange fruit" she is singing about? In what ways do you think it is strange?

Southern trees bear strange fruit,
Blood on the leaves and blood at the root,
Black bodies swinging in the southern breeze,
Strange fruit hanging from the poplar trees.
Pastoral scene of the gallant south,
The bulging eyes and the twisted mouth,
Scent of magnolias, sweet and fresh,
Then the sudden smell of burning flesh...

3. Community Learning

The whole class is divided into several groups proposing feasible plans for environmental protection. Each group is expected to use rhetorical techniques to persuade others. The audience will judge each group's proposal and ask each speaker relevant questions to test the feasibility of his/her plan. The plan is decided by voting.

Teachers may record students' performance and let them watch afterwards and ask the speakers to evaluate their own performance.

Part Four
English Speaking Contest

Unit 25

Prepared Speech in English Speaking Contests

> Speak properly, and in as few words as you can, but always plainly; for the end of speech is not ostentation, but to be understood.
>
> — William Penn[1]

Unit Goals

- To learn some basics of an English speaking contest
- To learn how to prepare a speech based on a given topic
- To deliver a prepared speech
- To learn how to judge a prepared speech

Warm-Up

1. If you enter an English speaking contest, what would be your major purpose?
2. Speaking to win is different from other forms of speaking. What do you think are the differences?
3. How important do you think the judges are in a speaking contest? How important do you think it is to appeal to the judges?

Knowledge Input

Preparing to Speak to Win

As China is now playing a greater role in the international community, the need for English speaking is becoming greater, too. In recent years, in order to encourage students to speak better English, various English speaking contests have been organized all over China at various levels. Many students consider entering an English speaking contest a big event in their college life, and value the experience very much. More and more universities are also making greater efforts in order to win in such contests.

In most English speaking contests, there will be a prepared speech based on a given topic. You can expect the prepared speech to be persuasive in nature; therefore, all the methods you have learned in the previous units can be of help to you in preparing the speech. Here are some additional tips to help you win.

Know the audience and occasion. In a speech contest, the audience will be your fellow students, your teachers, the media — and most important of all — the judging panel, which is usually a combination of both Chinese and foreign teachers and experts. The occasion for the contest is often quite formal. If you do not want to mess up your chance of standing on the stage, make sure you dress up properly and say and do everything in the spirit of the event. It will be difficult to appeal to each and every one of the judges, but you should try to avoid politically sensitive content and other explosive issues so as not to cause any feelings of discomfort on the audience's part. Be careful with jokes and humor. Make sure they are dignified and "safe" in content. You can be critical or emotional, but at the same time be positive.

Decide on a point you feel strongly about. Usually, the topic, or the subject matter of the speech, is very broad. It is advisable that you narrow the topic down to a more manageable perspective. If you know or feel deeply about this perspective, you surely will have something to say about it — that would be your central point or purpose. Make it creative if you can. You should state your point clearly in a powerful statement, which is to be restated and echoed throughout the speech. Only by doing so can your speech achieve unity and coherence. For example, if you get the topic "The future is now", your perspective may be education, environment, or investment. Choose one you feel very strongly about, decide on your point, and speak from the bottom of your heart. This is where your passion will come from.

Do research for your speech and use a variety of support. No matter how much you know about the topic, your knowledge may still prove inadequate for a convincing speech. To use resources and do research work is a must in preparing a speech. The resources you can use include books, newspapers, magazines, and the Internet. Once you start the research work, you will find a variety of supporting details that may be of your service —

stories, reports, examples, statistics, metaphors, images, quotations, etc. Specific, vivid details will add both interest and credibility to your speech. Without these, your speech cannot escape from being superficial and therefore lose its rhetoric value.

Use simple structure. The wisdom and beauty of your speech should be conveyed mostly through content, while structure can remain straightforward. The "point — support — summary" form will work fine for most speeches. A tricky or loose structure is against the basic rule of speech rhetoric because it will easily confuse audience.

Polish your language. Get whatever help you can to improve the English in your script. Use shorter words and plain English to highlight the content and rhythm of your speech. Replace words that are difficult to pronounce with simpler, brisker ones. Also avoid lengthy, tricky quotes that are difficult to understand.

Practice your delivery. The prepared speech is the only part of a contest that you have total control over. Spare no efforts to practice delivering it. Practice it as if you were practicing singing a song — leaving nothing out including your *breathing, pitch, tone, pause, stress, rhythm, facial expression, eye contact, pose, body language, microphone manners*, etc. Ask your teachers and fellow students to be your audience and judges. Listen to their feedback and suggestions until you achieve "studied naturalness".

Let your personality shine. Winning or losing is not just about the few minutes on the stage. It is more about the person that you are. Be confident in the person that you are, and you will shine on the stage.

Knowledge Internalization

1. Solo Work

The following are some of the topics for a prepared speech in major national English speaking contests. Decide on the perspective and point for each one.

1) The Future is Now
2) Unity and Diversity
3) The Global Me
4) Our Changing Way of Living with the Times: Initiative vs. Convenience
5) My Other Self

2. Pair Work

Exchange your perspectives and points with your partner. Is there any diversity?

Explain to your partner your purpose and learn from each other.

3. Solo Work

Use the perspective and point you have decided on and complete the following task.

1) Write a statement stating your point.
2) Use different resources to do research work for your purpose.
3) Plan a simple outline for your speech. In your outline, you should include the statement of your point and major supporting details.

Comprehensive Input

The following is the script of the unedited speech made by the 8th "21st Century Cup" champion Gu Qiubei[2].

Good afternoon, ladies and gentlemen,

Today I would like to begin with a story. There was once a physical therapist who traveled all the way from America to Africa to do a census about mountain gorillas. These gorillas are a main attraction to tourists from all over the world; this put them severely under threat of poaching and being put into the zoo. She went there out of curiosity, but what she saw strengthened her determination to devote her whole life to fighting for those beautiful creatures. She witnessed a scene, a scene taking us to a place we never imaged we've ever been, where in the very depth of the African rainforest, surrounded by trees, flowers and butterflies, the mother gorillas cuddled their babies.

Yes, that's a memorable scene in one of my favorite movies, called Gorillas in the Mist, based on a true story of Mrs. Diana Fossey, who spent most of her lifetime in Rwanda to protect the ecoenvironment there until the very end of her life.

To me, the movie not only presents an unforgettable scene but also acts as a timeless reminder that we should not develop the tourist industry at the cost of our eco-environment.

Today, we live in a world of prosperity but still threatened by so many new problems. On the one hand, tourism, as one of the most promising industries in the 21st century, provides people with the great opportunity to see everything there is to see and to go any place there is to go. It has become a lifestyle for some people, and has turned out to be the driving force in GDP growth. It has the magic to turn a backward town into a wonderland of prosperity. But on the other hand, many problems can occur — natural scenes aren't natural anymore. Deforestation to heat lodges are devastating Nepal. Oil spills from tourist boats are polluting Antarctica. Tribal people are forsaking their native music and dress to listen to U2 on Walkman and wear Nike and Reeboks.

All these appalling facts have brought us to the realization that we can no longer stand by and do nothing, because the very thought of it has been eroding our resources. Encouragingly, the explosive growth of global travel has put tourism again in the spotlight, which is why the United Nations has made 2002 the year of ecotourism, for the first time to bring to the world's attention the benefits of tourism, but also its capacity to destroy our ecoenvironment.

Now every year, many local ecoenvironmental protection organizations are receiving donations — big notes, small notes or even coins — from housewives, plumbers, ambulance drivers, salesmen, teachers, children and invalids. Some of them cannot afford to send the money but they do. These are the ones who drive the cabs, who nurse in hospitals, who are suffering from ecological damage in their neighborhood. Why? Because they care. Because they still want their Mother Nature back. Because they know it still belongs to them.

This kind of feeling that I have, ladies and gentlemen, is when it feels like it, smells like it, and looks like it, it's all coming from a scene to be remembered, a scene to recall and to cherish.

The other night, as I saw the moon linger over the land and before it was sent into the invisible, my mind was filled with songs. I found myself humming softly, not to the music, but to something else, someplace else, a place remembered, a place untouched, a field of grass where no one seemed to have been except the deer.

And all those unforgettable scenes strengthened the feeling that it's time for us to do something, for our own and our coming generation.

Once again, I have come to think of Mrs. Diana Fossey because it is with her spirit, passion, courage and strong sense of our ecoenvironment that we are taking our next step into the world.

And no matter who we are, what we do and where we go, in our minds, there's always a scene to remember, a scene worth our effort to protect it and fight for it.

Comprehensive Practice

1. Pair Work

Discuss the following questions with your partner.
1) What is the point of the speech? Is it clearly stated? Can you find restatements or echoes of this point in the speech?
2) Does the speaker use images/scenes and metaphors? What effect do the images

and metaphors create?

3) What different types of support does the speaker use?

4) In what way does the speaker make her structure complete and bring the speech to a natural, positive ending?

2. Group Work

Being passionate is a tricky thing in public speaking. Sometimes you may do it at the expense of spontaneity. If you overdo it, it may well backfire on you and ruin the whole speech.

Discuss with your group members:

1) In what way is this sample speech passionate?

2) What can contribute to the right kind of passion in public speaking?

Select a representative from your group to present your ideas to the class.

3. Solo Work

Compose a speech based on one of the topics in previous work in this unit.

4. Solo Work

1) Listen to Gu Qiubei's speech carefully and observe how the speaker controls her voice and language flow.

2) Read the speech aloud. Pay attention to voice control.

5. Solo Work

Practice delivering the speech you have composed. Pay attention to vocal skills and body language.

6. Class Work

Use your classroom as a small auditorium and each student deliver the speech he/she has composed based on the topics given. The whole class can be the judging panel. After all of the students have given their speeches, choose a best speaker to represent your class in the speech contest of your school.

Extra Input

Read the following unedited speech excerpts carefully and point out at least one outstanding feature in it. Learn to use it in your own speech.

1) Our ancestors liked to build walls. They built walls in Beijing, Xi'an, Nanjing and many other cities, and they built the Great Wall, which snakes through half of our country. I have to admit that we do have many walls in China, and as we are developing our country, we must carefully examine them, whether they are physical or intangible. We will keep some walls but tear down those that impede

China's development...

(By Xia Peng, champion of the 10th "21st Century Cup" English speaking contest)

2) If a person inherits his father's millions of dollars and leads an easy life, he is not a successful person even in material terms, because there are no difficulties involved in his achieving affluence. The term "success", to be sure, will not sit still for easy definition. But as I understand it, the true meaning of success entails a combination of both the process and the satisfactory result of an endeavor...

(By Chen Heng, champion of the 5th "21st Century Cup" English speaking contest)

3) What happened to this beautiful valley in Australia should also happen to our Yellow River and, in fact, it is happening. I have seen farmers planting trees on mountains along the Yellow River. I have seen them climb the mountain tops with seedlings on their shoulders because they had no machinery. I have seen them pour on trees the water they carried up in buckets from miles down the valley. These farmers are quietly nourishing our Yellow River, just as the river has nourished them...

(By Cai Li, champion of the 4th "21st Century Cup" English speaking contest)

New Hurdles

1. Retelling

Listen to the passage and retell it immediately after you have heard it.

The final contest of the 8th PKU (Peking University) Speech Contest will be held on Saturday, with 17 contestants qualified. They will demonstrate their feelings and thoughts with their various personalities and presentations on the theme of "2048".

Judges of the final contest are: Prof. Yan Buke, Prof. Sun Qixiang, Prof. Wu Guosheng, Mr. Zhuang Yongzhi, chief editor of "JiaoDianFangTan" (Focus Talk), and Mr. Wang Yongbin, Editor-in-Chief of People Daily. All members of the judging panel are experts with profound comprehension of public speaking and vast experience in giving speeches. It is expected that this group will give some marvelous remarks on the contest.

International students also took part in the contest. Their performances have already won a lot of applause. International students who are qualified for the final say that they are preparing for the final moment carefully. An American student will bring us a speech entitled "Cats in PKU", expressing his innovative idea on the theme "2048".

Contestants will be required to make an impromptu speech in the final. This will make the competition harsher and the event more attractive. Moreover, organizers of the final have prepared several gifts for the audience.

This final contest will open at 2:00 pm May 12th at Sunny Hall, Overseas Exchange Center. Tickets will be distributed at Old Biology Building during 12:30 to 14:30 on May 10th and 11th. Students can get the tickets by presenting their own student ID cards.

2. Talking on a Given Topic

You are required to talk about "Being passionate in public speaking" based on your knowledge and understanding of the topic. You can talk about being passionate in both composition and delivery. Make sure you are making sense by giving reasonable suggestions. You have three minutes to prepare your talk and then give it to your partner.

3. Role Play

The task involves two students, Student A and Student B. Each has a specified role as follows. Although the situation is the same, your roles are different. Learn about the role you want to play. Your preparation time is three minutes. Your conversation is limited to four minutes.

Student A: You are doing research work for your speech. You want to know how to use resources and what resources can be used for various needs. You need to find statistics, examples, quotes, metaphors, etc. for your speech. You ask Student B for help. Remember you should start the conversation.

Student B: You are to offer suggestions to Student A concerning the use of resources in doing research work for a speech. Tell him/her what each type of resource can be best used for. The resource may include books, magazines, newspapers, the Internet, etc. Discuss both the advantages and disadvantages of these resources.

Notes

1. William Penn (1644 – 1718): an early champion of democracy and religious freedom. He was known as the first great hero of American liberty.
2. The 8th "21st Century Cup" English speaking contest was held in 2003 with the theme "Tourism and Ecology: Learning Through Travel". Gu Qiubei, champion of the contest, was a student from Shanghai International Studies University. Her speech in the contest has been widely studied and quoted.

Amusement Park

1. Movie to Enjoy

See the following movie and share your personal view with your classmates next week.

Philadelphia (1993)

The movie tells the story of Andrew Beckett (Tom Hanks), an easygoing senior associate at the largest law firm in Philadelphia. Beckett hides his homosexuality and his status as a person living with AIDS from the other members of the law firm. When he is fired on false charges, he hired a homophobic lawyer Joe Miller (Denzel Washington) to sue his former law firm for wrongful dismissal…

The movie won Academy Awards for Best Actor in a Leading Role (Tom Hanks) and Best Music (Bruce Springsteen for "Streets of Philadelphia").

Special Highlight

The movie *Philadelphia* is full of wonderful court cross-examination scenes, in which the prosecutor, the defense lawyer, and the witnesses all gave memorable presentations or testimonies. In one of the cross-examinations, Tom Hanks tells what he loves most about being a lawyer: You get to be part of justice… being done.

Court scenes are very good for imitation exercises. Select a team of lawyers and witnesses and imitate and perform one of the court scenes. Videotape your performance and then show it to your classmates.

2. Song to Enjoy

The following is part of the lyrics to the song "Streets of Philadelphia" by Bruce Springsteen. Find a recording of the song, listen to it and complete the lyrics.

What mood are you in when you listen to the song? How do the music and the lyrics fit into the movie?

> I was bruised and battered and I couldn't tell
> What I felt
> I was unrecognizable to myself

I saw my reflection in a window I did not know
My own face
Oh brother are you gonna leave me
Wasting away
On the streets of Philadelphia...
The night has fallen, I'm lying awake
I can feel myself fading away
So receive me brother with your faithless kiss
Or will we leave each other alone like this
On the streets of Philadelphia...

3. Community Learning

Watch the DVD of the "CCTV Cup" English Speaking Contest in your dorm room. Select your favorite speaker (he/she does not have to be the winner), and give your comment on his/her performance. Your comment should include both his/her strengths and weaknesses.

Unit 26

Impromptu Speech in English Speaking Contests

> It usually takes more than three weeks to prepare a good impromptu speech.
> — Mark Twain

Unit Goals

- To find out what impromptu speech is
- To learn what type of topics are usually used for impromptu speech in a contest
- To learn how to plan an impromptu speech
- To learn to deliver an impromptu speech

Warm-Up

1. Do you think most major speaking contests should include an impromptu speech?
2. What strengths or weaknesses may be demonstrated in an impromptu speech?
3. Many contestants say the impromptu speech is the most intimidating part of the competition. How come? What is so difficult about it?

Knowledge Input

Planning an Impromptu Speech

Before taking on the task of planning an impromptu speech, it is necessary that you know the basic rules. In major speech contests, what happens is that 15 or 30 minutes before your turn to go on the stage, you get to choose the topic for your impromptu speech. Then you have 15 or 30 minutes to prepare. When it is time for you to step onto the stage, you first give the prepared speech, directly followed by the impromptu speech you just prepared, and the Q & A session.

The topics for impromptu speeches may range from personal to cultural, or campus issues to current affairs. However, they mostly fall into three categories: topical issues, interpretation of quotes, and commentaries on pictures, videos or props.

The impromptu speech is the most challenging part of a speech contest because you get the topic "out of the blue", and you need to be able to stay calm and think on your feet. Then you need to talk coherently on one topic for 3 minutes! Since the impromptu speech accounts for a large part of your final score (40% or more), it largely determines whether you can win or not.

In planning your impromptu speech, following the simple steps below and you'll find the task much more manageable.

Make sure you understand the topic. It is essential that you understand the quote, the video or the issue being discussed correctly. If you come across a new word, use the dictionary provided. Spend a minute to digest the topic.

Develop a clear point. Think about how you react to the topic and settle on one major point or stand. Jot down a few key words, a turn of phrase, or a neat statement to express your point. Keep this point in your mind. Your speech is going to evolve around this point and this statement.

Work out an outline. Determine several major subpoints that you want to cover and search your mind for necessary supporting details to discuss each subpoint clearly and concisely. Keep the ideas flow clear and logical by using markers such as "first", "next", "finally", etc. These markers identify each point and help the audience keep track of your thoughts. A sample outline is given below:

Lead-in → Statement of point → Sub-point 1 → Support 1 → Sub-point 2 → Support 2 → Sub-point 3 → Support 3 → Ending.

Let's see an example made by Dong Bo, a finalist in the 2007 "CCTV Cup". Her topic was: Should our cities be expanding outwards or upwards? She first stated her central point clearly by saying: "I firmly believe that cities should be expanding upwards. I have three points to back up my argument." Then she went on to explore the three points — land, communication, and management — one by one, using "first of all", "secondly" and "thirdly" to mark them clearly. Finally, she restated her central point to bring the speech to a positive, strong ending. At no point did she stray off course. There is nothing flashy or ostentatious in the organization, but it is very clear, very effective indeed.

While you are preparing, just jot down a few key words or phrases to indicate the points and support, and let yourself see the organization. There's no need to prepare a script.

Have an effective beginning and ending. Maybe you can not completely avoid rambling or faltering in the middle of the speech, but make sure that you have a very neat, effective beginning and ending. In the beginning, let the audience know what you are going to say; in the ending, bring the audience back to your point, or restate your point in a stronger note.

Keep good timing. You usually have 3 to 4 minutes for your impromptu speech. Using up your time without stating all your points is devastating to your speech. In your training,  you must learn to have a clear idea how much you can say within 3 minutes. Do not get involved in a lengthy story. Keep your examples concise and to the point.

 *Look confident.* Try to look calm and confident regardless of how nervous you might feel. Keep a reasonable pace; do not speak too fast or use too many vocalized pauses. Maintain your composure and talk in an assured manner, and you will make a good impression on the audience and the judges.

Work to be a winner off stage. Again, a brilliant impromptu speech is not just the work of the few minutes on the stage. It takes a lot of accumulation of knowledge and experience to make a competent speaker. In the end, what really counts is how much you already have in your head when you need it.

Knowledge Internalization

1. Pair Work

Discuss the following questions with your partner.

1) Why is it necessary to have a central point or stand in an impromptu speech?
2) Why is it advisable to use markers such as "firstly", "lastly", etc. when giving an impromptu speech?
3) In what aspects are prepared speech and impromptu speech alike? In what aspects are they different?

2. Solo Work

The following are some impromptu speech topics used in speech contests. Do you find them difficult?

Choose one and give yourself 15 minutes to work out an outline for the speech.

Quotes

1) One flower is beautiful, but a surfeit is vulgar.
2) A person does not only want to be rich; he/she wants to be richer than others.

Topical issues

3) Will online shopping replace traditional shopping?
4) Why do you think such competitions shows like "American Idol" and "Super Girls" have attracted so many people?

Video, picture or props

5) Comment on a cartoon: A son asks his mother in her car, "Mum, why can't I walk to school?" "Cos there's too much traffic."
6) Comment on the object you have — an umbrella.

3. Group Work

Form groups of four and share your outline with your group members. Choose the best outline, improve it, and then present it to the class.

Comprehensive Input

The following is an impromptu speech made by Liu Yiran, grand finalist of 2006 "CCTV Cup". (The speech is not edited.)

Topic: A recent "Charming Teacher" contest was launched in Xuzhou, aimed to select the "Top 10 Charming Teachers". What, in your opinion, are the charms of a teacher?

Well, the first thing flashing in my mind when I saw this topic was the Super Girls Contest, which is very hot this year in China. But as the English saying goes, "we can not judge a book by its cover", so I do not think that we can judge the charming teachers only by their appearance. There are a lot of charming teachers sitting here today, including the judges and all the teachers here. But I think the common characters of the charming teachers are the following four.

The first one is, as a teacher, he or she should be knowledgeable both theoretical and practical. The ancient teacher in China, the most famous one Confucius, traveled a lot and he teaches his students by a lot of practical examples, like he said, "Tough policies are worse than tigers." That is because he saw in the ancient times there are a lot of tough policies and he taught his students by examples not only in classes.

The second character of a charming teacher should be patience. A charming teacher should never be bored by students' endless questions. And he should spend time with students, discuss with them, and this was what the ex-president of Peking University Mr. Cai Yuanpei did. He encouraged students to discuss, to create and to innovate.

The third character is a good teacher should be kind and considerate. He or she should always have a gentle attitude, should smile and understand the difficulties of students and try to help them to solve the problems. Like I'm standing here today instead of taking my calculus examination which is on my schedule, and my teacher just agreed I came here to take part in this competition. And this is what I consider a charming teacher. He is very considerate.

The fourth one is a good teacher should have good ways to teach each student according to each individual. A teacher should not teach such a large class and everybody in the same way. He or she should have one way to teach each student. That does not necessarily mean that he should teach each student individually, and teach each individual student a lesson. But he or she should guide them individually. So I have such teachers at school. Every time I go to the library she is sitting there, burying her head in books and doing research. She is all self, organizing party for her students. And so that is what I consider a charming teacher to be.

Thank you very much.

Comprehensive Practice

1. Solo Work

Read the speech carefully and then watch the video.

2. Group Work

Form groups of four or five. Each group is responsible for exploring one of the following questions. Then each group should choose a spokesperson to present your comments to the class.

1) How does he appeal to the audience and judges? Do you think he achieved his purpose?
2) Does he have one clear central point? Is this point effectively stated?
3) Are the examples he uses to the point?

4) How did he build up his credibility?

5) What are the speaker's major merits in terms of delivery?

3. Class Work

Encourage several students to volunteer to deliver an impromptu speech they have just prepared. The speaker may take the outline onto the stage as a reminder of the ideas and structure.

After the speaker finishes, the class should comment on his/her performance.

4. Solo Work

If you have not had the chance to speak in front of the class, give yourself a challenge and deliver your own impromptu speech in front of the mirror. See if you can keep talking meaningfully for 3 minutes. Or you can ask your friends to be your supportive audience and give you feedback after you finish.

Extra Input

Read the following speech excerpts (beginning and ending) carefully and point out at least one outstanding feature in it. Learn to use it in your own speech.

1) Thomas Jefferson once said, "I'm a great believer in luck, and I find the harder I work, the more I have of it." What, though, is luck? Webster's Dictionary suggests that luck is the "events or circumstances that operate for or against an individual". In truth, luck has nothing to do with something operating for or against you. Luck is not a matter of chance; it is a matter of being open to new experiences, perseverance and hard work, and positive thinking.

2) As long as discrimination and inequities remain so commonplace everywhere in the

world, as long as girls and women are valued less, fed less, fed last, overworked, underpaid, not schooled, and subjected to violence in and outside their homes, the potential of the human family to create a peaceful, prosperous world will not be realized.

Let this conference be our — and the world's — call to action. Let us heed that call so we can create a world in which every woman is treated with respect and dignity, every boy and girl is loved and cared for equally, and every family has the hope of a strong and stable future. That is the work before you. That is the work before all of us who have a vision of the world we want to see — for our children and our grandchildren.

The time is now. We must move beyond rhetoric. We must move beyond recognition of problems to work together, to have the efforts to build that common ground we hope to see.

(Hillary Clinton, U. N. Women's Conference in Beijing, 1995)

New Hurdles

1. Retelling

Listen to the passage and retell it immediately after you have heard it.

The 14th National English Speech Contest has attracted two million college students since its online preliminary selection began three months ago.

The competition is jointly sponsored by *China Daily* and the Lenovo Group. The theme for this year's competition is "The City and Quality of Life". Topics of the speeches may cover city construction, environment protection, communication, as well as social problems brought about by urbanization.

The competition will have four stages: first is the preliminary selection online, and then there will be an oral test via phone, regional contests, and at last the final contest, which will be held in April.

Now at the first stage, contestants can submit their readings of English stories, poems, film scripts and even songs to the official website. The public are invited to vote for talented contestants either online or through mobile phone messages.

Learning English has become a fashion since China adopted its reform and open policy 30 years ago. In recent years, English skill has become a necessary quality to get a good job. Yet, for a long time, English teaching in China emphasized reading and writing rather than listening and speaking; therefore, students could easily get high scores despite poor spoken English.

To improve the situation, China began to change the English teaching methods in 2002 by emphasizing oral communication. The competition is also one way to encourage Chinese schools to improve communication-oriented teaching methods of English.

2. Talking on a Given Topic

You are required to talk about the advantages and disadvantages of online shopping vs. shopping in the physical world. Keep your ideas well organized. You have three minutes to prepare your talk and then give it to your partner.

3. Role Play

The task involves two students, Student A and Student B. Each has a specified role as follows. Although the situation is the same, your roles are different. Learn about the role you want to play. Your preparation time is three minutes. Your conversation is limited to four minutes.

Student A: You are going to enter an English speaking contest and you do not feel very confident in yourself. Student B has been in the same contest last year and you talk to him/her about your feelings of uncertainty. Ask him/her about the experience last year and try to learn something from the conversation. Remember you should start the conversation.

Student B: You took part in the English speaking contest last year and entered the final. This year's contestant — Student B — talks to you for he/she does not feel sure about himself/herself. Tell him/her about your experience last year and answer his/her questions. Be positive and encouraging.

Amusement Park

1. Movie to Enjoy

See the following movie and share your personal view with your classmates.

A Few Good Men (1992)

This movie is a dramatic courtroom thriller. Daniel Kaffee (Tom Cruise) is an inexperienced U.S. Navy lawyer. He leads the defense in the court-martial of two Marines who are accused of murdering a fellow Marine of their unit at the Guantanamo Bay Naval Base in Cuba. The two accused are suspected that they, who were top-class Marines, were carrying out a "code red" ordered by Colonel Nathan Jessup (Jack Nicholson), the C.O. of the Marine detachment at Guantanamo Bay...

Special Highlight

Like *Philadelphia*, *A Few Good Men* is also full of wonderful courtroom cross-examination scenes, and the court scenes are added with a military touch. What is most unforgettable is Colonel Nathan Jessep addressing the court on "Code Red". Nicholson's reading of the line "You can not handle the truth!" was voted the twenty-ninth greatest American movie quote of all time by the American Film Institute.

What is "Code Red"? Why is it so disturbing?

How do you like Jack Nicholson's performance? Are you convinced of his evil? Or are you touched by his dignity?

2. Song to Enjoy

The following is part of the lyrics to the song "To Be Number One" by Giorgio Moroder.

Find the song, listen to it and complete the lyrics.

Do you feel motivated by the song? Observe how the singer uses his voice and body to influence the audience. You can also learn to use your voice in singing to build up your vocal expressiveness!

> This is what we've worked for all our lives
> Reaching for the highest goal we can
> We choose to give it all
> When competition calls
> Time records the victory in our hearts
> To win or lose is not the only thing
> It's all in how we play for the fairest game
> This is the chance we take
> Reaching for the top
> Time records the victory in our hearts
>
> To be number one...
> Running like the wind
> Playing hard but always playing fair...

3. Community Learning

Watch the video of "CCTV Cup" English Speaking Contest. Try to find the same speaker doing both prepared speech and impromptu speech. Do you see any differences in their performance? If you see any differences, what are they? Discuss with your classmates what may have caused the differences.

Unit 27

Q & A in English Speaking Contests

> It is not the answer that enlightens, but the question.
> — Eugene Ionesco[1]

Unit Goals

- To learn about the Question-and-Answer session in speech contests
- To learn how to prepare for the Q & A session
- To learn how to answer a question in the right manner of delivery

Warm-Up

1. Do you like watching the Q & A session? What do you think is most exciting about it?
2. Some contestants can give ingenious answers to the questions asked. Do you think they have correctly predicted the questions beforehand? Or is it because they are smart enough to formulate the best answer offhand?
3. The Q & A session usually accounts for about 30% of the final score. Do you think it is too much?
4. Do you feel some questions in the Q & A session are more difficult than other questions? Do you think the Q & A session can be made completely fair?

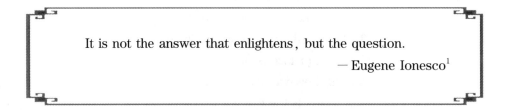

Knowledge Input

Question-and-Answer Session

After the contestant has finished both the prepared and impromptu speeches, the question masters will usually ask them two questions — one concerning the prepared speech, the other concerning the impromptu speech. Contestants must answer each question right away, having no time to think or prepare. The Q & A session is designed to test the contestants' quick response, and their ability to organize language and thoughts on the spot.

The questions can be the least you expect. Actually, the question masters' job is to device the least predictable questions based on the speeches to catch you off-guard. So do not count on luck. But there are ways to come off nicely in this most interesting and challenging part of the contest and make you shine uniquely.

First, study your own prepared speech script carefully and get ready for whatever may come. Of course you cannot be sure what the questions may be, but you can explore the possibilities and design answers that may apply to a range of questions. Invite your teachers and friends to help you by asking you pop questions. By doing so, you not only expand the content of your speech, but also equip yourself with more knowledge and ideas. When the real test comes, you will have much more up your sleeves to help you get through.

Concentrate on the impromptu speech itself rather than the questions when preparing it. Some contestants use one or two minutes to think about possible questions when they

are preparing the impromptu speech, but this is usually not worth it. For the question may be anything the question master thinks of when he/she is listening to you. The best policy is to stay calm and take whatever question comes your way. Make sure your answer is crisp, straightforward and to the point. Draw on your speech and restate your major points when they apply. Improvise to the best of your ability. You may end up saying things that will even surprise yourself!

Listen to the questions carefully. You need to make sure what the questions are about in order to answer them right to the point. If you feel the question is unclear, you may paraphrase it and say, "If I understand your question correctly, you seem to be asking…" Or you may simply say "I beg your pardon?" The question masters are very gracious people and they will repeat the question for you. Never blunder into an answer without knowing the question.

Answer the question the way you give a speech. Some students only look at the question master when answering questions, forgetting that this is still part of the speech. Your audience will lose you if you stop having eye contact with them, and your wonderful answers are lost to them, too. Address the entire room and complete your answer on a confident note.

Respond to the question directly and watch your time limit. The questions are to be answered within one minute, so practice to make your answers brief and to the point. Beating about the bush is no way of avoiding a tough question. Elaborating on unnecessary or irrelevant details (because you know how to say them!) will kill your point. Although the judges do not expect perfect answers, they appreciate answers that directly address the questions.

Build up your knowledge reserve and language reserve. As the Chinese saying goes, you only know you have too little knowledge when you need it. In the Q & A session, you surest and biggest support is your own reserve — the work done before and outside the competition. Winning or losing is not determined by the few minutes on the stage; it is determined long before.

Knowledge Internalization

1. Pair Work

Study the speeches your partner has used in the previous units and design three questions based on each. Then discuss with your partner possible answers to the questions. Note down the questions and brief answers.

2. Group Work

In the Q & A session, many contestants say "Thank you for your question" before they answer it. Maybe they say this in order to win the valuable two seconds to organize their thoughts, or maybe they say it out of a habit.

Discuss with your group the following questions and then present the results of your discussion to the class.

1) Is it appropriate or necessary to say "Thank you for your question"? Why or why not?
2) If you want to have a few seconds' hesitation or thinking time, what else can you say or do without losing grace?

Comprehensive Input

The following are two examples of the Q & A taken from the semifinal of the 2007 "CCTV Cup" English Speaking Contest. (The answers are not edited.)

1) *Question Master:* You told a story of your mother and plastic bags. ... If you were a

plastic bag, what would you say to people?

Wang Liansi: I'm a plastic bag. I really should not be given birth to in this world. I regret someone ... I regret having been invented because I'm a disaster. But now I'm already invented, what can I do? I do not want to die; I just want to find a place for me to sleep, to exist and to live a peaceful life. Well, I know how much you people hate me, but what can you do? I will not decay in a million years; I  will not decay when the earth disappears. So I will always stay here. No matter what you do, I will be that evil, wicked plastic bag. This is what I, if I were a plastic bag, would say. So if any human being heard what I have said, you should be alarmed, and we should be alarmed, because this is the nature of plastic bags. They are harmful. They will not decay. They will continue to be a nightmare to humankind. Thank you.

2) *Question Master*: Just quickly, can you help me with the meaning of Yin and Yang?
Dai Yuerong: Just quickly... Yang refers more to the male side and Yin is the female side.
Question Master: If you take Chinese and western culture, which would be Yin and which would be Yang? And why?

 *Dai Yuerong*: I think it is a combination because every culture has its Yin side and has its Yang side. And I have to add a little bit because Yin and Yang doesn't only refer to the female and male side of the culture, but also the weaker side and the stronger side, or the brighter side and maybe the not so bright side. So I think for every culture, it has its Yin side and Yang side. So when we are combining the two sides together, then we'll have a complete and fully flourishing culture. I think that is the advantage of every culture, because it has its uniqueness, it has different portion in its Yin side and Yang side, but the combination is very important.

Comprehensive Practice

1. Solo Work

If possible, watch the DVD to observe the overall performance of the speaker.

2. Pair Work

Discuss the following questions with your partner.

1) What do you think of the questions? In what ways do you think they are most challenging?
2) Comment on the answers and point out the strengths and weaknesses.

3. Pair Work

Use the questions and answers you have discussed in Knowledge Internalization and deliver the answers to you partner. Ask your partner to observe your performance and give suggestions.

4. Pair Work

Design one fresh question based on your partner's speech and ask the question. Your partner should answer the question immediately. Then discuss the question and the answer and do it again.

5. Class Work

Do a mock Q & A by having several volunteers come to the front of the classroom and deliver a speech. Then the class can ask them questions based on their speeches. Comment on their performance and choose the best answer.

Extra Input

The following are two excerpts of the Q & A transcripts between a journalist and a political leader. Study them carefully and see how the questions are tactfully and effectively answered.

Which answer do you like better? Do you prefer Ms. Clinton's directness and sharpness or do you prefer Premier Wen Jiabao's gentle, modest wisdom?

1) *Question by Michael Tomasky*: Do you think that the terrorists hate us for our freedoms, or do you think they have specific geopolitical objectives?

   Answer by Hillary Clinton: Well, I believe that terrorism is a tool that has been utilized throughout history to achieve certain objectives. Some have been ideological, others territorial. There are personality-driven terrorist objectives. The bottom line is, you can not lump all terrorists together. And I think we've got to do a much better job of clarifying what are the motivations of terrorists. I mean, terrorists may not share all that much in terms of what is the philosophical or ideological underpinning. And I think one of our mistakes has been painting with such a broad brush, which has not been particularly helpful in understanding what it is we were up against...

   (October 23, 2007)

2) *Question by Fareed Zakaria*: Let me ask you a final question, Your Excellency. You must have been watching the American election. What is your reaction to the strange race and election that we are having in this country?

Answer by Wen Jiabao: The presidential election of the United States should be decided by the American people. But what I follow very closely is the relationship between China and the United States after the election. In recent years, there has been a sound growth momentum in the growth of China-U. S. relations. And we hope, whoever is elected as the president and whoever is sworn into the White House, no matter which party wins the election, that he or she and the parties will continue to grow the relationship with China. And China hopes to continue to improve and grow its relationship with the United States no matter who will take office and lead the new administration in this country.

(September 29, 2008)

New Hurdles

1. Retelling

Listen to the passage and retell it immediately after you have heard it.

My Job Interview

I arrived at Meritus Hotel about 20 minutes ahead of the interview time, and the receptionist showed me to its meeting room. The 20 minutes was precious to me because it allowed me some time to recollect and calm down. Actually, I was reciting my English self-introduction on the bus because I just learnt it would be an English interview the previous night.

When it came to 10 o'clock, the manager came in. Before asking me any questions, she impressed me with her fluent English by giving me an introduction of their company and the major responsibilities of the position I was applying for. I got used to her accent and speed, so I had no great difficulty understanding her.

She first asked me to give a self-introduction. It was no big deal because I had done enough preparation. She seemed to be pleased with my introduction.

After the self-introduction, she asked me some more questions. Most questions were the common interview-type ones, and they were not hard to answer. I just took it as a casual talk with a friend, so I was more like telling vivid stories to her. She seemed to be interested in my stories.

There was just one question that was a little special. The question was: What was the something you have devoted most to but finally failed to get? When I tried to remember, I was not quite sure what I said in response to it. But I was sure that I said something like

"It is the experience that counts." or that sort of thing. But judging from the manager's positive response, I must have said the right thing.

2. Talking on a Given Topic

You are required to talk about your understanding of the following quote: *"It is possible to be different and still be all right. There can be two — or more — answers to the same question, and all can be right."* First state your opinion concerning the quote and then give reasons to back up your opinion. You have three minutes to prepare your talk and then give it to your partner.

3. Role Play

The task involves two students, Student A and Student B. Each has a specified role as follows. Although the situation is the same, your roles are different. Learn about the role you want to play. Your preparation time is three minutes. Your conversation is limited to four minutes.

Student A: You are a reporter with the student union newsletter. You are going to interview a renowned professor in your university. The questions you ask may include his academic achievements, excellent students he's had, his hobbies and interests, etc. You discuss the questions to be asked with your editor to make sure that they are appropriate. Remember you should start the conversation.

Student B: You are the editor-in-chief of the student union newsletter. One of your reporters is going to interview a renowned professor in your university. Discuss with him/her what questions to ask so that the interview will be interesting to read. Give suggestions when you can and bring the conversation to a fruitful ending.

Notes

1. Eugene Ionesco (1909 — 1994): Romanian and French playwright and dramatist. He was one of the foremost playwrights of the Theatre of the Absurd. Ionesco's plays often depict the solitude and insignificance of human existence.

Amusement Park

1. Movie to Enjoy

See the following movie and share your personal view with your classmates next week.

Crimson Tide (**1995**)

This is the most severe nuclear crisis after the Cold War. Russian rebels have taken over a nuclear missile site and are refueling them for a possible strike against the United States of America. On the U. S. nuclear missile submarine Alabama, a young first officer Ron Hunter (Denzel Washington) stages a mutiny to prevent his trigger happy captain Frank Ramsey (Gene Hackman) from launching his missiles before confirming his orders to do so…

Special Highlight

In the movie, both Captain Frank Ramsey and first officer Ron Hunter have addressed the crew of the USS Alabama. Their speeches represent different attitudes toward the use of force, and different types of patriotism. When Denzel Washington steps out of the courtroom and into a submarine, he acquires a different kind of power.

Both good and evil can find their voice in speeches. How can we assure that the voice of good is always louder?

2. Song to Enjoy

The following is part of the lyrics to the song "Whatever Will Be, Will Be" by Doris Day. Find a recording of the song, listen to it and complete the lyrics.

Is it always easy to answer a little kid's questions about life and nature? Why is it sometimes most difficult to answer the most innocent question?

When I was just a little girl,
I asked my mother,
"What will I be?
Will I be pretty?
Will I be rich?"

Here's what she said to me:
"Que sera, sera,
Whatever will be, will be;
The future's not ours to see.
Que sera, sera,
What will be, will be."
...

3. Community Learning

Organize an English quiz show in your dorm. One of you will be the question master and the others are contestants. The question master is responsible for giving out 20 quiz questions and their answers in English. See who will be able to answer most questions. Prepare a gift for the winner.

Part Five
Debating Skills

Unit 28

Basics of Debate

> Freedom is hammered out on the anvil of discussion, dissent, and debate.
>
> — Hubert Humphrey[1]

Unit Goals

- To learn about the differences between debate and other argument or persuasion techniques
- To understand the values of studying debate activities
- To learn about various types of debates
- To learn the etiquettes in debating

Warm-Up

1. Why do you think people ever need to debate?
2. Do you sometimes disagree with a classmate on something? How do you resolve the disagreement? Does the disagreement affect your relationship in any way?
3. Have you found any effective ways in your experience when debating?

Knowledge Input

Debate: What and Why?

As an English learner, we are all familiar with the term "debate", either from presidential election debates or various international English debating competitions. How much do you know about debate and why do we need to learn it?

Debate, in its simplest form, is an exchange of

reasoned arguments for and against a proposition. In educational debate or factual debate, the end result is determined by evaluating the cogency of each side's arguments. Public debate should give priority to logic while maintaining awareness of emotional appeals, whereas propaganda is an organized campaign of persuasion, and it is characteristically one-sided. In some cases, the opposing side may be explained, but only in a distortion or as a straw man.

In debates, there are three basic types of proposition: *fact, value, and policy.*

A debate of fact always follows this form: The affirmative side states that a certain thing is true while the negative maintains that it is false. Note that "false" is the status quo. The debate is automatically won by the negative unless the positive produces enough factual, scientific data to prove his statement.

A debate of value is one in which the positive maintains that a certain thing is good, and the negative claims that it is either neutral or bad. It is important to understand that without a properly defined basis for goodness or badness, any argument is doubtful. Therefore, something must be identified as good with regard to something else, based on other properly defined criteria. This type of debate, while more subjective, still holds to the rule that the negative position wins by presumption if a competent case is not presented by the positive speaker.

Policy debate is slightly different than value debate. Again, the positive side maintains that a certain action should be adopted while the negative asserts that it should not. The subtle difference here is that there is no imperative that a policy be good by any set standard. In other words, this is where good is weighed against greater good. This is obviously the least objective style of debate, and is usually left to political topics.

Whatever the type, we all hope to debate in order to get closer to the truth, or make better decisions. But as students, what benefits can we get from debating activities? The following are some quotes from successful people about debate as an educational activity. We can see the values of debate not only in terms of language skills but also concerning its mind uplifting.

John F. Kennedy[2] commented, "I think debating in high school and college is most valuable training, whether for politics, the law, business, or for service on community committees such as the PTA and the League of Women Voters. A good debater must not only study material in support of his own case, but he must also, of course, thoroughly analyze the expected argument of his opponent. The give and take of debating, and the testing of ideas, is essential to democracy. I wish we had a good deal more debating in our educational institutions than we do now."

"He learns to use a library, and to find the exact information he needs in the shortest possible time. He learns to be thorough and accurate. He learns to analyze, to distinguish between the vital and the unimportant. He learns the need of proving his statements, of supporting every statement with valid evidence and sound reasoning; and he learns to demand the same sort of proof for the statements of others. He learns to present ideas in a clear and effective manner, and in a way which wins others to his way of thinking. He learns to think under pressure, to 'use his head' in a time of need, to make decisions quickly and accurately." Summers[3] argued. So it is not quite exaggerating to say that debate is probably the ultimate "mind exercise".

Knowledge Internalization

1. Solo Work

Search the Internet or other media for three different definitions of "debate" and sum them up with your own explanation of the term.

2. Pair Work

Discuss with your partner about the following questions.
1) In persuading someone, what techniques or strategies can you think of that people may use?
2) What is the difference between debate and other argument forms, and why?

3. Group Work

Divide the class into three groups. Each is assigned respectively the task of working out propositions of fact, value and policy. Then select a representative to report it to the class.

4. Class Work

Answer voluntarily the open question "What benefits can we have by exercising our debating skills?"

Lexical Power Build-Up

1. Starting a Debate

Here are some useful language chunks for starting a debate. Practice them until you can say them automatically, but pay special attention to their pronunciation and intonation.

Today we are debating the topic...

I was wondering where you stood on the question of...
Group A will be on the pros and Group B on the cons.
On the affirmative side we have Team A, and on the negative side we have Team B.
I would like to propose a solution to the problem we are facing.
Gentlemen, at this very moment tonight, where do you stand on...?

2. Agreeing and Disagreeing

Here are some useful language chunks for agreement and disagreement. Practice them until you can say them automatically, but pay special attention to their pronunciation and intonation.

1) How to agree strongly with an opinion.
I couldn't agree more.
That's absolutely true!
I'd go along with you there.

2) How to half agree with an opinion.
Yes, perhaps, however...
Yes, I agree up to a point, however...
Well, you have a point there, but...

3) How to disagree politely with an opinion.
Well it depends.
Hmm, I'm not sure you're right.
I'm inclined to disagree with you.

4) How to disagree strongly with an opinion.
I disagree with your idea.
I couldn't accept that for a minute.
It's possible you are mistaken about that.

3. Solo Work

Make up complete sentences in a creative way using the expressions, and then practise them orally.

4. Group Work

In groups of three — the affirmative, the negative and the "moderator" — create your propositions and supporting ideas, and practise using the language chunks listed above.

Comprehensive Input

Debate Topic: Arranged Marriages

Arranged marriages make up the vast percentage in human history but have, largely in the last century, become unusual and morally questioned in the world. The following are some opposing opinions about the question "Should arranged marriages be outlawed"?

Pros

The practice of arranged marriage separates communities, helping to stop integration and encourage distrust between communities. This applies largely where it occurs among immigrant populations and helps to maintain a language barrier and even a cultural isolation. This doesn't just create a group of people who can feel trapped between two cultures and unsure of whether they have a place in their host society, but a poverty trap associated with the language barrier that creates further segregation. It also helps to foster distrust in the wider community by holding to such a radically alien value, particularly where it is opposed to our notion of equal rights.

Cons

It is not just groups practicing arranged marriage who maintain cohesive communities. Afro-Caribbean and Jewish people in Western Europe both maintain a distinct cultural life while taking part fully in the life of this country. In fact their cultural contributions are one of the most valuable additions to the societies in which they live. The basis of multiculturalism is to understand the social and even economic value that can accrue from having people with different perspectives and traditions living together. Furthermore, in the second and third generations of immigrant families from the subcontinent we can already see barriers breaking down so that there is greater understanding and cross-fertilization of the ideas these immigrant communities have brought.

Pros

Arranged marriage is not a true "cultural value" that is in some sense inviolate. Every major religion including Islam guarantees the legitimacy of freedom of choice in marriage. Further, the extent to which this is custom is a product of a patriarchal culture that oppresses women and maintains the imbalance of power between the genders. Although we cannot intervene in countries that hold to such a value system, we can stop such a system being imported. True multiculturalism itself relies on some basic shared value of commitment to a tolerant and fair society.

Cons

Both young and old people affirm the fact that arranged marriage is a cultural tradition and any ethnographic data confirms it, not to mention the frequency of arrangement throughout the world. As we have pointed out, there is no conflict between arrangement and a guarantee of free choice, the two are entirely consistent. Who is going to stand up and tell ethnic minorities that they do not know whether they want arranged marriages and whether or not it really is part of their culture? Furthermore, how can we possibly insist that immigrants respect our virtues of "tolerance" if that amounts to denying them cultural freedom?

...

Comprehensive Practice

1. Pair Work

Discuss whether the above arguments are convincing enough. Are there any strong emotional appeals or inappropriate persuasion or propaganda used in them?

2. Pair Work

Recite the pros and cons and practice presenting them to each other orally. Pay attention to your manners, for example, keeping calm and rational, keeping good pace, etc.

3. Solo Work

Prepare a short speech on "Should Computer Games on Campus Be Banned?" Your position can be assigned and it can be of your own choice as well.

4. Group Work

In groups of four, share your speech with each other and decide on the "strongest" evidence for your position.

5. Class Work

Under the management of the assigned moderator, practise a team debate. The moderator will give clear introduction to the occasion so that the audience knows clearly what's going on. Then the whole class will evaluate either side's performance.

Extra Input

The following is an excerpt of the classic debate on the "Existence of God" between Frederick Copleston (C) and Bertrand Russell (R).

Note how the ideas engage each other and how the speakers defend their own stand.

C: Cause is a kind of sufficient reason. Only contingent being can have a cause. God is His own sufficient reason; and He is not cause of Himself. By sufficient reason in the full sense I mean an explanation adequate for the existence of some particular being.

R: But when is an explanation adequate? Suppose I am about to make a flame with a match. You may say that the adequate explanation of that is that I rub it on the box.

C: Well, for practical purposes — but theoretically — that is only a partial explanation. An adequate explanation must ultimately be a total explanation, to which nothing further can be added.

R: Then I can only say that you're looking for something which can not be got, and which one ought not to expect to get.

C: To say that one has not found it is one thing; to say that one should not look for it seems to me rather dogmatic.

R: Well, I do not know. I mean, the explanation of one thing is another thing which makes the other thing dependent on yet another, and you have to grasp this sorry scheme of things entirely to do what you want, and that we can not do.

C: But are you going to say that we can not, or we shouldn't even raise the question of the existence of the whole of this sorry scheme of things — of the whole universe?

R: Yes, I do not think there's any meaning in it at all. I think the word "universe" is a handy word in some connections, but I do not think it stands for anything that has a meaning.

New Hurdles

1. Retelling

Listen to the passage and retell it immediately after you have heard it.

Experience vs. Degree

Whether it is a completely strategic discussion about your organization's policies or a discussion involving a specific position and candidate, this issue continually resurfaces at organizations. And depending on what side of the fence you sit, this issue can be very personal and emotional. Do a quick Internet search, and you'll find a common theme. Your search results will be dominated by links to chat/message boards where someone who has many years of applicable work experience but no degree poses a question about how to further his or her career without getting a degree. Of course, the question is followed by endless responses debating the issue.

Obviously, there are specific cases where the question is debatable. If you need a registered professional engineer to approve plans, the degree requirement is a given. If you're a hospital looking for a surgeon, you're probably seeking someone with a PhD in medicine. However, the scope of positions that may or may not require a degree gets gray pretty fast, and the span is pretty wide. And, no industry is immune to this issue.

I've helped draft more job descriptions than I care to admit, and each time I ask the question of whether or not a degree is required, the response is usually based on cultural or personal preferences. Ironically, the hiring manager often justifies the decision to require a degree on "experience".

2. Talking on a Given Topic

You are required to talk about your experience of debating or arguing with someone, for example, friends or classmates or parents over certain issues. You have three minutes to prepare your talk and then talk to your partner. You may talk about the process, your gains, your analysis or comment, etc.

3. Role Play

Staying up late is common among young people, which worries many parents. Act out a brief debate between an affirmative, Student A, and a negative side, Student B, over the question "Does staying up late at night do harm to college students?" Your preparation time is three minutes. Your debating time is limited to four minutes.

Student A: Your role is to do the pros of the topic as a parent would do. First you will think of very strong evidence to support your opinion about the harms of staying up late. Then try to criticize in advance possible negative argument. Remember to do it with good manners and in a rational and convincing way. Remember you should start the debate by stating your point.

Student B: Your role is to do the cons of the topic as a "night owl". First you will think of very strong evidence to support your opinion against the proposition about staying up late. Then try to criticize in advance possible affirmative argument. Remember to do it with good manners and in a rational and convincing way.

Notes

1. Hubert Humphrey (1911 – 1978): the 38th U. S. Vice President under Lyndon Johnson (1965 – 1969) and U.S. Senator from Minnesota (1949 – 1964, 1971 – 1978)
2. John F. Kennedy (1917 – 1963): the 35th President of the United States

3. Harrison Boyd Summers: author of the textbook for beginners *How to Debate*

Amusement Park

1. Movie to Enjoy

See the following movie and share your personal view with your classmates next week.

300 (2006)

300 tells the story of the Battle of Thermopylae in 480 B.C. Persians under the rule of King Xerxes have already taken over some of the Hellenic city-states, and now threaten Sparta and Athens. King Leonidas of Sparta is left with two options: he will either have to sacrifice himself for the well-being of Sparta or watch it burn to the ground. Choosing the former, Leonidas forms an army of 300 Spartan warriors to block the narrow passage of Thermopylae where Xerxes intends to reach Hellas...

Special Highlight

Dilios's stirring motivational speech to his Spartan warriors before the Battle of Plataea is particularly memorable. The finest Spartan soldiers are aware of their fate, but are motivated by "honor and glory".

How does the word "victory" impress you? What would your talk of victory be like?

2. Song to Enjoy

Complete the lyrics while you are enjoying the song "No Matter What" by Boyzone.

What belief do you think the song expresses? Do you think the message is made powerful enough?

No matter what they tell us
No matter what they do
No matter what they teach us
What we believe is true
No matter what they call us
However they attack
No matter where they take us
We'll find our own way back

I can't deny what I believe
I can't be what I'm not
I know our love forever
I know no matter what
...

3. Community Learning

The monitor and study monitor will invite some students to work together to design a debate activity. They may divide the class into two camps, design the motion for the debate and assign their classmates different tasks, such as gathering material, organizing a team, creating speeches, etc. Then the two camps should stage a debate, with the monitor and study monitor serving as moderators for the event.

Unit 29

Evidence for Debate

> If it is a disgrace to a man when he cannot defend himself in a bodily way, it would be absurd not to think him disgraced when he cannot defend himself with reason in a speech.
> — Aristotle[1]

Unit Goals

- To learn the importance of the use of evidence in debating
- To learn about different kinds of evidence to use in debate
- To learn to support your opinion with appropriate evidence

Warm-Up

1. If someone told you that you were employed by your dream company, what would you like him to prove it with: Another friend told him so? A photo copy of the company's e-mail notice? Or an official notice with the company's seal?
2. Explain to yourself why you trust the evidence you have chosen and not the other evidence.
3. Suppose you are to convince someone of a similar piece of news without the "hard evidence", the official letter, how would you try to do it?

Knowledge Input

Supporting Your Opinion with Evidence

Evidence is the heart of any debate, the deciding factor in court, the raw material for argumentation.

Evidence can be put into various kinds. There is direct evidence and presumptive evidence. Direct evidence is evidence that is sufficient to demonstrate the fact in question without the need to question any of the supporting facts. In a debate about the legality of abortion, a simple reference from the Supreme Court records would establish without question that the case was decided between 1971 and 1973. No further fact checking is necessary, and it is not necessary to establish the credibility of the Supreme Court records. Direct evidence seldom supports the proposition, for if there were such direct evidence, the proposition would hardly be debatable. So, direct evidence appears almost exclusively in support of contentions.

Presumptive evidence, also known as indirect or circumstantial, is evidence that tends to demonstrate a fact in question by inference. Clearly, presumptive evidence is not as strong as direct evidence, and when the two are at odds, direct evidence always prevails. Suppose that someone claimed to see a UFO over the White House at 6 p.m., on Friday. Suppose further that this person was a congressman, and a well trusted confidant of the President. Suppose that in addition, several of his most trusted aides were with him, and also claim to have seen the UFO. This could be considered strong circumstantial evidence, and a debate might well end with the conclusion that there was a UFO over the White House. However, if there was file tape from Friday, with a direct, panoramic view of the sky over the White House, and no UFO appeared, the direct evidence would prevail, and the conclusion would have to be that there was no UFO over the White House.

Then there is primary and secondary evidence. Primary evidence is original evidence. The original text of a book, an actual fossil, or a bloody knife would all be considered primary evidence. This is the most certain kind of evidence, and is always favored over secondary evidence. Secondary evidence is anything that is not primary. Third generation copies of an ancient text or a photo of a fossil are examples of secondary evidence. Clearly, secondary evidence carries much less weight, and demands far more confirmation before it can be considered strong enough to carry a proposition.

Real evidence and personal evidence is another classification. Real evidence is essentially objects that demonstrate a claim. Fingerprints, scars, maps, and videotapes are all real evidence. Since it is extremely

difficult to argue against the existence of something that is sitting on a table in front of you, real evidence is some of the strongest evidence in any debate. It must be noted that real evidence can be used to support any part of an argument or proposition. In other words, the argument that there is such a thing as a beetle that looks just like an ant would be directly proven by the presence of just such a beetle in a display case for everyone to see. The proposition under debate, however, might be the evolutionary path taken by animals which mimic other animals. In this case, the beetle would be just one of many pieces to a much larger puzzle. Personal evidence, as the name implies, is any evidence provided by a person. As you might expect, personal evidence is considered very weak unless there is convincing real evidence.

Knowledge Internalization

1. Pair Work

Retell the passage with your partner and reinforce the understanding of the content on the kinds of evidence.

2. Solo Work

If you have a proposition "Our teacher is a very responsible teacher", brain-storm a list of about 10 pieces of evidence which may support your opinion.

3. Pair Work

Now discuss with your partner to first rearrange the order of the list according to their convincing power. Then figure out what category each evidence falls into.

Lexical Power Build-Up

1. Lexical Input

Here are some useful language chunks for debate. Practice them until you can say them automatically, but pay special attention to their pronunciation and intonation.

Do you have a response to this?
I wonder if you could explain that, sir?
How do you justify the act of...?
Do you consider these sufficient reasons for...?
How would you go about enacting this plan?
Given these conditions, the concept of... is unintelligible.
To use a common example...
I have direct evidence to prove...
Let's take a look at these official statistics and do the math.

Let me show you a piece of evidence to prove...

A host of examples and incidents will support me in saying...

There is no denying that...

It is hasty and inconsiderate to base your point on one story.

2. Solo Work

Make up complete sentences using the useful expressions and rehearse them.

3. Pair Work

Think of a debatable issue on campus and argue from opposite sides. Try to use the expressions above as much as possible.

Comprehensive Input

The following is part of the 1960 presidential debate on the issue of education, between Kennedy and Nixon[2]. Note how Kennedy raised his education plans, how Nixon responded to the plans and how Kennedy rebutted Nixon's response.

Kennedy:

I'm not satisfied when many of our teachers are inadequately paid, or when our children go to school in part-time shifts. I'm not satisfied until every American enjoys his full constitutional rights. If a Negro baby is born — and this is true also of Puerto Ricans and Mexicans in some of our cities — he has about one-half as much chance to get through high school as a white baby. He has one-third as much chance to get through college as a white student...

Nixon:

Federal funds must be used for school construction, not for paying teachers. Once the Federal government assumes responsibility for paying a portion of teachers' salaries, your state and local communities are not going to meet the responsibility that they should. Let me make this clear: I do not object to the cost in dollars. I object to giving the Federal government power over education, which is the greatest power a government can have. We must keep massive programs like the one Senator Kennedy suggests out of our educational system in order to preserve our teachers' freedom to teach as they wish.

Kennedy:

I support Federal aid to education and Federal aid for teachers' salaries. I think that's a good investment. I think we're going to have to do it. And I think to heap the burden further on the property tax, which is already strained in many of our communities, will ensure, in my opinion, that many of our children will not be adequately educated, and many of our teachers not adequately compensated.

Comprehensive Practice

1. Solo Work

Recite the Kennedy vs. Nixon debate, paying attention to the language they used.

2. Pair Work

Recite the exchanges between Kennedy and Nixon. Then take turns to act out their parts.

3. Group Work

In groups of three or four, discuss the evidence used in the above presidential debate.

4. Group Work

We all know that we can contribute to our economic development by spending more money. But as college students without an income, can we still do it? Divide the class into two sides, and plan to debate the proposition "College students can spend more money in many ways". Both sides should brainstorm for evidence to support their stand.

5. Class Work

Both sides from the activity above select a representative team to participate in the real debate. Audience on either side may provide help, such as fresh evidence, to their team by slipping notes to their representatives. Attention should be paid to language use, logic, attitude, etc.

Extra Input

Read the following speech excerpt carefully and see how the speaker expresses herself at this.

Speech at the 54th Annual Emmy Awards
Oprah Winfrey

...There really is nothing more important to me than striving to be a good human being. So, to be here tonight and be acknowledged as the first to receive this honor is

beyond expression in words for me. "I am a human being, nothing human is alien to me." Terence said that in 154 B. C., and when I first read it many years ago, I had no idea of the depth of that meaning.

I grew up in Nashville with a father who owned a barbershop, Winfrey's Barbershop, he still does, I can not get him to retire. And every holiday, every holiday, all of the transients and the guys who I thought were just losers who hung out at the shop, and were always bumming haircuts from my father and borrowing money from my dad, all those guys always ended up at our dinner table. They were a cast of real characters — it was Fox and Shorty and Bootsy and Slim. And I would say, "Bootsy, could you pass the peas please?" And I would often say to my father afterwards, "Dad, why can not we just have regular people at our Christmas dinner?"— because I was looking for the Currier & Ives version. And my father said to me, "They are regular people. They're just like you. They want the same thing you want." And I would say, "What?" And he'd say, "To be fed." And at the time, I just thought he was talking about dinner. But I have since learned how profound he really was, because we all are just regular people seeking the same thing. The guy on the street, the woman in the classroom, the Israeli, the Afghani, the Zuni, the Apache, the Irish, the Protestant, the Catholic, the gay, the straight, you, me — we all just want to know that we matter. We want validation. We want the same things. We want safety and we want to live a long life. We want to find somebody to love. We want to find somebody to laugh with and have the power and the place to cry with when necessary.

The greatest pain in life is to be invisible. What I've learned is that we all just want to be heard. And I thank all the people who continue to let me hear your stories, and by sharing your stories, you let other people see themselves and for a moment, glimpse the power to change and the power to triumph.

Maya Angelou said, "When you learn, teach. When you get, give." I want you to know that this award to me means that I will continue to strive to give back to the world what it has given to me, so that I might even be more worthy of tonight's honor.

Thank you.

New Hurdles

1. Retelling

Listen to the passage and retell it immediately after you have heard it.

One of the criticisms I have heard about Disney's tales is that they are "sugar-coated". If that means "not showing the nitty-gritty" of the story, I'm not sure that's true. It's quite clear that Cinderella and Snow White are treated badly and are unloved by their wicked stepmothers. And it is quite clear that the stepmothers are wicked. They are jealous, petty, cruel or even downright evil. There are scary, insecure moments like when Snow White is lost in the forest or when the Beauty is confronted by the Beast. I have to be honest, too — I do some of my own sugar-coating. I might say that Snow White's stepmother died alone and forgotten, but I may not give the original ending where it describes  how at the wedding she was given red-hot iron shoes in which she was forced to dance until she fell down dead. I think many of the tough messages in the stories are still there in Disney's films.

Another criticism of these versions is that the story is changed. But haven't these stories changed from the time they were first spoken or written down? Haven't the stories changed as they were carried from one culture to another? Do not present-day storytellers change stories according to their own interpretation and style? I imagine there are as many versions of *Cinderella* in this country as there are versions in different cultures. My daughter was even given a version in which the illustrations are photos of those big, gray dogs dressed in costume to portray the characters. When I tell stories, I may prefer not to change what I have found to be the basic plot and details of a particular story, but Disney is not the only one to have altered a traditional tale.

2. Talking on a Given Topic

You are required to talk about your opinion about the value of the practice trip to Disneyland as a junior English major. You have three minutes to prepare your talk and then talk to your partner.

3. Role Play

The task involves two students (if necessary, invite a moderator), Student A and Student B. Each has a specified role indicated below. Learn about the role you want to play. Your preparation time is three minutes. Your conversation is limited to four minutes.

Student A: You are supposed to argue for the opinion that females make better language learners than males. Make use of any knowledge, experience and observation to support your opinion.

Student B: Your role is to argue against the opinion that females make better language learners than males. You should make use of any knowledge, experience and observation to rebut the affirmative side. You do not have to prove that males are better language learners.

Notes

1. Aristotle (384BC—322BC): Greek philosopher.
2. Richard Nixon (1913—1994): the 37th President of the United States, from 1969 to 1974.

Amusement Park

1. Movie to Enjoy

See the following movie and share your personal view with your classmates next week.

The Shining (1980)

"All work and no play makes Jack a dull boy"—or, rather, a homicidal boy in Stanley Kubrick's eerie 1980 adaptation of Stephen King's horror novel. With wife Wendy (Shelley Duvall) and psychic son Danny (Danny Lloyd) in tow, frustrated writer Jack Torrance (Jack Nicholson) takes a job as the winter caretaker at the opulently ominous, mountain-locked Overlook Hotel so that he can write in peace. Before the Overlook is vacated for the Torrances, the manager (Barry Nelson) informs Jack that a previous caretaker went crazy and slaughtered his family. Jack thinks it's no problem, but Danny's "shining" hints otherwise. Settling into their routine, Danny cruises through the empty corridors and plays in the topiary maze with Wendy, while Jack sets up shop in a cavernous lounge with strict orders not to be disturbed. As Danny is plagued by more blood-soaked visions of the past, a blocked Jack starts visiting the hotel bar for a few visions of his own. Frightened by her husband's behavior and Danny's visit to the forbidding Room 237, Wendy soon discovers what Jack has really been doing in his study all day, and what the hotel has done to Jack...

Special Highlight

It is interesting to notice how Jack Nicholson changes and controls the quality of his voice when he speaks. The way he speaks contributes much to the effect of the movie as well as the characterization of the leading role.

Try to imitate some of his lines and see whether you can adjust your own voice.

2. Song to Enjoy

Learn to sing the following song and sing it to the class, best with music. The following is part of the lyrics. Complete the lyrics before you perform.

Girls usually want their boyfriends to be strong and brave, but how do boys want their girlfriends to be?

Hero

by Enrique Iglesias

Would you dance,
If I asked you to dance?
Would you run,
And never look back?
Would you cry,
If you saw me crying?
And would you save my soul, tonight?

Would you tremble,
If I touched your lips?
Would you laugh?
Oh please tell me this.
Now would you die,
For the one you love?
Hold me in your arms, tonight.

I can be your hero, baby.
I can kiss away the pain.
I will stand by you forever.
You can take my breath away.

...

3. Community Learning

What is the currently most hotly debated policy issue on your campus? Does the university authority feel the same way as the students do on this issue? Form two groups to represent the administration and the student body. Debate and negotiate. Try to reach a solution.

Unit 30

Logic in Debate

> Reasoning and logic are to each other as health is to medicine, or — better — as conduct is to morality. The very reason we need logic at all is because most reasoning is not conscious at all.
> — Julian Jaynes[1]

Unit Goals

- To learn basic logic in argument
- To learn what a good argument is like
- To learn about some common logical fallacies

Warm-Up

1. In the 2000 election, when a reporter would question Bush about his reputed past drug use and drinking, he said, "When I was young and stupid, I was young and stupid." Does this make sense to you? Why do you think he talked like that?
2. Do you know how logic basically works, with premises and conclusion?
3. Note how the following argument uses logic: Johnny is a good hitter. Why is he a good hitter? Because he has a high batting average. Why does Johnny have a high batting average? Because he is a good hitter. How would you comment on the use of logic in such reasoning?

Knowledge Input

Arguing with Logic

In logic, an argument is an attempt to demonstrate the truth of an assertion called a conclusion, based on the truth of a set of assertions called premises. The process of demonstration of deductive and inductive reasoning shapes the argument, and presumes some kind of communication, which could be part of a written text, a speech or a conversation.

An argument is a controversial statement, frequently called a claim, supported by evidence and a warrant. The standards of a logically good argument include acceptability, relevance, and sufficiency. Hence, argumentation is the uniquely human use of reasoning to communicate. The structure of an argument can be diagrammed to illustrate various types of arguments. So, there are simple argument structure, convergent argument structure, and independent argument structure. Understanding argument structure is especially important in the world of educational debate, which highlights the way an understanding of argument structure is useful for not only debate competitions, but also youth advocacy, and cooperative problem solving.

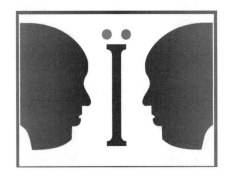

In evaluating an argument, we consider separately the truth of the premises and the validity of the logical relationships between the premises, any intermediate assertions and the conclusion. The main logical property of an argument that is of concern to us here is whether it is truth preserving; that is, if the premises are true, then so is the conclusion. We will usually abbreviate this property by saying simply that the argument is valid.

If the argument is valid, the premises together entail or imply the conclusion. The ways in which arguments go wrong tend to fall into certain patterns, called logical fallacies.

One way to start the analysis and evaluation of arguments is the "informal fallacies" device. It stresses the important connection between logical argumentation and logical fallacies. A quality argument upholds the RSA Triangle, of Relevance, Sufficiency, and Acceptability. That is, a quality argument is understood by the relationship between its two component parts, the premise(s) and the conclusion. Specifically, a quality argument upholds the standard of relevance, the standard of sufficiency, and the standard of acceptability. Therefore, a fallacy is "a pattern of argumentation that violates one of the criteria a good argument must satisfy and that occurs with some marked degree of frequency".

Another way to look at good arguments is the four-criterion category. A good argument must have premises that are relevant to the truth of the conclusion, premises that are acceptable, premises that constitute sufficient grounds for the truth of the conclusion, and premises that anticipate and provide an effective rebuttal to all reasonable challenges to the argument or to the position supported by it. An argument that meets all of these conditions is a good one, and its conclusion should be accepted.

Regardless of the number of categories, when assessing an argument, one must chart the quality of the link between the conclusion and its premise(s). A weak link between a conclusion and its premise(s) often indicates a fallacy.

Some types of fallacies include the following: argument ad hominem, ambiguity, appeal to fear, appeal to popularity, appeal to tradition, begging the question, equivocation, fallacy of composition, fallacy of division, fallacy of incompatibility, faulty analogy, hasty conclusion, improper appeal, loaded term, poisoning the well, post hoc fallacy, problematic premise, red herring, slippery slope argument, straw person fallacy, two wrongs fallacy, and vagueness.

Knowledge Internalization

1. Solo Work

Search the Internet or other media for information on the three stages of an argument: premises, inference and conclusion. Then work out three arguments by using this format.

2. Pair Work

Exchange with your partner your arguments and discuss whose are more convincing.

3. Group Work

In groups of four, distribute the above-mentioned fallacies to the members, each of whom will be responsible for learning about five fallacies. Then discuss these fallacies with examples. Try to find out why they are problematic.

Lexical Power Build-Up

1. Lexical Input

Here are some useful expressions when reasoning. Practice them until you can say them automatically, but pay special attention to their pronunciation and intonation.

On the grounds that..., we know that...
What follows from these facts is obvious — we need/should...
The statistics allows us to infer that...
Your argument suggests very strongly that you neglected a very critical problem.
Our conclusion may be inferred from all the phenomena in society.
His rational analysis bears out the point that this theory is problematic.
In view of the fact that..., we should...
These facts indicate that...
My opinion may be deduced from those results.
The above analysis points to the conclusion that...

2. Solo Work

Practice speaking the above expressions fluently until you can say them automatically. Make up your own sentences in a creative way and practice them orally.

3. Pair Work

Prepare three 3-step reasoning examples. Use the expressions above. Exchange with your partner and discuss which ones sound more valid.

Comprehensive Input

The following is an excerpt from a presidential debate between Obama and Clinton on the issue of health care. According to Obama's plan, health insurance should be voluntary, not mandatory as proposed by Clinton's plan. One concern is that there might be about 15 million people who would still not be covered. Here is how he argues for his plan.

Obama: Well, understand who we're talking about here. Every expert who looks at it says anybody who wants health care will be able to get health care under my plan. There won't be anybody out there who wants health care who will not be able to get it. That's point number one.

So the estimate is — this is where the 15 million figure comes in — that there are 15 million people who do not want health care. That's the argument.

Now, first of all, I dispute that there are 15 million people out there who do not want it. I believe that there are people who cannot afford it, and if we provide them enough subsidies, they will purchase it.

Number two, I mandate coverage for all children.

Number three, I say that young people, who are the most likely to be healthy but think they are invulnerable — and decide I do not need health care — what I'm saying is that insurance companies and my plan as well will allow people up to 25 years old to be covered under their parents' plan.

So, as a consequence, I do not believe that there will be 15 million out there.

Now, under any mandate, you are going to have problems with people who do not end up having health coverage. Massachusetts right now embarked on an experiment where they mandated coverage.

And, by the way, I want to congratulate Governor Schwarzenegger and the speaker and others who have been trying to do this in California, but I know that those who have looked at it understand, you can mandate it, but there's still going to be people who cannot afford it. And if they cannot afford it, then the question is: what are you going to do about it?

Are you going to fine them? Are you going to garnish their wages?

You know, those are questions that Senator Clinton has not answered with respect to her plan, but I think we can anticipate that there would also be people potentially who are not covered and are actually hurt if they have a mandate imposed on them.

Comprehensive Practice

1. Solo Work

Read the excerpt carefully and critically.

2. Pair Work

Discuss and analyze how Obama uses logical argument in defending his health care plan, and whether it is convincing.

3. Solo Work

Recite the excerpt, and practice presenting it orally. Try to be articulate in the ways of manners, pace, pauses, as well as pronunciation and intonation, etc.

4. Group Work

Search for and study some sample debates and sort out a few typical arguments and analyze if they are logical or of invalid inference. Then share your research findings with other groups in your class.

5. Solo Work

Under the global economic crisis, what is your strategy in coping with it? Put down your argument for your choice and make sure it is logical and free of fallacies.

6. Group Work

Present your strategy to your group members and exchange your thoughts within the group. Help each other decide which arguments are stronger than others.

Extra Input

Read the following debate excerpt carefully and see how the debaters made their point clear and how they used logic to support their argument.

Debate on the Existence of God Between Frederick Copleston(C) and Bertrand Russell(R) (Excerpt)

C: As we are going to discuss the existence of God, it might perhaps be as well to come to some provisional agreement as to what we understand by the term

"God". I presume that we mean a supreme personal being — distinct from the world and creator of the world. Would you agree to accept this statement as the meaning of the term "God"?

R: Yes, I accept this definition.

C: Well, my position is the affirmative position that such a being actually exists, and that His existence can be proved philosophically. Perhaps you would tell me if your position is that of agnosticism or of atheism. I mean, would you say that the non-existence of God can be proved?

R: No, I should not say that; my position is agnostic.

C: Would you agree with me that the problem of God is a problem of great importance? For example, would you agree that if God does not exist, human beings and human history can have no other purpose than the purpose they choose to give themselves?

R: Roughly speaking, yes, though I should have to place some limitation on it.

C: Would you agree that if there is no God — no absolute Being — there can be no absolute values? I mean, would you agree that if there is no absolute good that the relativity of values results?

R: No, I think these questions are logically distinct. Take, for instance, G. E. Moore's *Principia Ethica*, where he maintains that there is a distinction of good and evil, that both of these are definite concepts. But he does not bring in the idea of God to support that contention...

C: Well, for example, "T. S. Eliot exists"; one ought to say, for example, "He, the author of *Murder in the Cathedral*, exists." Are you going to say that the proposition, "The cause of the world exists" is without meaning? You may say that the world has no cause; but I fail to see how you can say that the proposition that "the cause of the world exists" is meaningless.

R: Well, certainly the question "Does the cause of the world exist?" is a question that has meaning. But if you say "Yes, God is the cause of the world", you're using God as a proper name; then "God exists" will not be a statement that has meaning. Because, therefore, it will follow that it cannot be an analytic proposition ever to say that this or that exists. For example, suppose you take as your subject "the existent round-square", it would look like an analytic proposition that "the existent round-square exists", but it doesn't exist...

New Hurdles

1. Retelling

Listen to/read the passage and retell it immediately after you have heard/read it.

I Thought She Was Great

Former President Bill Clinton was in high spirits as he took to the stage in Erie, Pennsylvania, eager to talk about what he thought of his wife's performance at ABC News' Democratic debate last night in Philadelphia.

"So, I want to begin by saying, I do not know if you saw that debate last night, but I did, and I thought she was great. She was great because she showed the strength and leadership and knowledge of the issues that is very important to the next president, and she did not hedge, beat around the bush on tough questions like Iran; she told us what she was gonna do on health care, she told us what she was gonna do on jobs. That's what you want in a president. Someone who is leading for you," Clinton told the crowd on the campus of Erie University of Pennsylvania.

Clinton went on to sprinkle debate references throughout his 45 minute speech, at one point saying he thought her answer on Iran was excellent as well. Joining the former president on the stump today is a longtime friend and Hillary Clinton supporter, Ted Danson. Danson's glowing description of Hillary during his introduction prompted Clinton to remind the crowd that the Hillary he knows is not the one he says has been created by the media and her opponent.

"I couldn't help thinking — I did not mean to start with this but I think I will. You heard what he said about Hillary? That's what the people who know her think. That is very different than the image that they have tried to create for her in the media, who are always nagging, nagging, nagging. You heard it for 15 months, you know? How come no one who knows her believes that?" Clinton asked the crowd, explaining that the people who really know her realize she is in it for the people.

Clinton is keeping a busy schedule today with 6 stops in some of the more rural and remote parts of Pennsylvania, including Warren and Lock Haven.

2. Talking on a Given Topic

You are required to talk about your opinion about the importance of logical argument in debating. You can support your opinion by showing some uses of fallacies. You have three minutes to prepare your talk and then give it to your partner.

3. Role Play

The task involves two students, Student A and Student B. Each has a specified role as follows. Although the situation is the same, your roles are different. Learn about the role you want to play. Your preparation time is three minutes. Your conversation is limited to four minutes.

Student A: You are a member of a debating team trying to defend the argument that "We should not follow the teacher's instructions when we do not agree with them". Remember to do it with logical argument, with valid evidence and inference. Remember you should start the debate by making the claim.

Student B: You represent the con team and give your argument against the proposition raised by the pro team. You will provide strong evidence to destroy it. If possible, find out the fallacies in your opponent's argument as one more way to use against your opponent.

Then, the two sides may respond to one another's argument for a few more rounds if time permits.

Notes

1. Julian Jaynes (1920 — 1997): American psychologist

Amusement Park

1. Movie to Enjoy

See the following movie and share your personal view with your classmates next week.

American Beauty (1999)

So this is what happens when the American dream turns sour. Director Mendes has really twisted the knife into American society with this dark comedy about love, hate, passion and murder.

Lester (Spacey) and his over-ambitious realtor wife Carolyn (Bening) used to be happy and in love, but now they hate spending time together and endure their lives for the sake of daughter Jane (Birch). On top of that, computer journalist Lester despises his employers, so when oddball neighbor Ricky (Bentley) re-introduces him to marijuana and teenage tease Angela (Mena Suvari) catches his eye, Burnham decides it's time for a change — with drastic consequences...

Special Highlight

Lester's monologue at the end of the movie is ranked "Top 10 pre-death monologues in film". It offers a really interesting window into Lester's philosophical look on life. It begins with "I had always heard your entire life flashes in front of your eyes the second before you die."

What do you feel when you listen to this monologue? Do you think it is true that when people are dying, they become kind and appreciative?

2. Song to Enjoy

The following is part of the lyrics to the song "Blue Night" by MLTR. Find a recording of the song, listen to it and complete the lyrics and learn to sing the song in English.

Do love songs always touch you? When you sing them, do you think of someone you are fond of?

> Lately you have been asking me
> If all my words are true
> Do not you know I'll do anything for you
> Sometimes I haven't been good to you
> Sometimes I've made you cry
> And I am sorry for everything
> But I promise you girl
> I promise you this
> When the blue night is over my face
> On the dark side of the world in space
> When I'm all alone with the stars above
> You are the one I love
> ...

3. Community Learning

Nowadays there is a hot debate going on whether high school students should be classified into "science students" and "art students". There are people and educators who believe the division of science and liberal arts classes in senior high school should be ended, while others think students' personal interest and overall academic burden should be taken into consideration before any change is made.

What is your stand? Divide the class into two camps and hold a debate using the topic "Should science and arts be one?" Note down each side's opinion and then find out which side has a stronger case.

Unit 31

Questioning and Team Skills in Debate

> Coming together is a beginning.
> Keeping together is progress.
> Working together is success.
> — Henry Ford[1]

Unit Goals

- To learn team debate skills
- To learn questioning techniques in debate
- To learn rhetorical language in debate

Warm-Up

1. In your school experience, can you recall a debate, either in Chinese or English, in which you beautifully co-operated with your team members? How did you co-operate?
2. You all may have noticed that skilled debaters sometimes ask a series of questions of their opponent. What do you think is the purpose of asking questions?
3. What kind of language do you feel can be most effective and impressive in a debate? Can you think of an example of powerful language in debate?
4. What special language skills have you learned from various debates?

Knowledge Input

Cross Examination Skills

In cross examination debate, the most important concern of the questioner is to create a positive impression on the audience. Questions in cross examination debate are very

different from those in Parliamentary debate. In Parliamentary debate, only a single question may be put, and it carries the burden (either through humor or straight refutation) of making a point. That is very difficult to do. In cross examination debate, however, a whole series of questions may be asked, and by seeking information a little bit at a time, a much more substantial point may be made. There is a more important reason for asking questions in a series: your purpose is to convince the audience; if you jump around, you may lose them. By asking questions in a series you let the audience follow your line of thought, and understand the purpose of the questions. You allow the judges to recognize your ability to think logically. And by focusing on three or four important lines of questioning, you signal to the judge that you can distinguish between important and trivial matters.

One of the most powerful questioning techniques is the "leading questions". The most exciting and challenging aspect of a debate occurs when a properly prepared questioner skillfully asks leading questions of the alert respondent. This results in a high-drama cat and mouse game in which the heart of the debate, the clash, is most clearly articulated. Leading questions suggest the intended answer. They might not always force the respondent to give the intended answer, but they do tend to limit the areas of response. When a leading question is asked, it is more difficult for the respondent to avoid a direct answer or to engage in speech making. As a respondent, you must be on your toes. Leading questions are designed to get you to agree with something that will harm your case or help the questioner's case. However, it is a mistake to take the view that, in order to avoid falling into that trap, you should disagree with everything that the questioner asks you. If you do so you will quickly be seen to be denying the obvious truth, and you will instantly lose credibility in the eyes of the judges. A good questioner will ask a series of leading questions with a view to getting the respondent to agree with him/her for the first few questions. After lulling the respondent into a pattern of agreement, the questioner may pose a target question, hoping to have thrown the respondent off his/her feet, and have him/her agree before realizing what has been admitted to. Once the questioner has received the favorable answer, he/she will immediately move to a new line of inquiry, distracting the respondent, and forcing him/her to concentrate upon a different topic before he/she has an opportunity to elaborate upon his/her earlier, harmful, admission.

During both your cross-examination and that of your partner, valuable information is being obtained from your opponents. In order to demonstrate proper cross examination technique, you must be able to show the judges how you can make use of the admissions which both your partner and you have obtained. It is tempting to use the cross-examination period as the time at which you draw conclusions about the admissions you have obtained from the opposition, but that would be a mistake. Cross-examination is a time to ask questions, not to state conclusions. The time to draw those conclusions is during the refutation phase of a subsequent constructive speech, or during the rebuttal speech. Take care to utilize not only the admissions which you have obtained from your opponents, but also those which your partner obtained. This shows good teamwork. It emphasizes the strongest points made by both members of your team. When engaged in the rebuttal speech, only one member of the team is permitted to speak for the team. It is therefore essential that that person show the judges that both the speaker and his/her partner obtained critical evidence from the opposition and that it can be used to that person's team's benefit.

Knowledge Internalization

1. Pair Work

With sample "leading questions" found from the Internet or other media, discuss the use of leading questions in cross-examinations.

2. Pair Work

With the above information and sample debate excerpts that contain "cross-examinations", discuss how they are used. How would it be different if we ask one direct question to get a targeted answer?

Lexical Power Build-Up

1. Lexical Input

Here are some examples of cross examination questions. Practice them until you can say them automatically, but pay special attention to their pronunciation and intonation.

Do you firmly believe in what you have stated?

If yes, then please give me some concrete proofs!

If you have no concrete proofs, how can you be so firm in your beliefs?

Do you know that beliefs without sufficient proofs are called blind dogmatism?

How fast was the red car going when it smashed into the blue car? (*This question implies that the red car was at fault, and the word "smashed" implies a high speed.*)

How much will prices go up next year? (*This assumes that prices will go up next year.*)

What do you think about John Richards? Many people are opposed to him, by the way. (*Note the social coercion in this statement.*)

Would you prefer to live in Alba or in Barta, where the crime rate is very low? (*Note that the crime rate in Alba is not mentioned, but the link of low crime with Barta will still make it more desirable.*)

2. Solo Work

Practice speaking the above questions fluently until you can say them forcefully.

3. Pair Work

1) Discuss the effects of the questions in Lexical Power Build-Up.
2) Think of a proposition that you two disagree on and design a series of questions for each other to answer, and see how it works for both of you.

4. Group Work

Work in groups of four and try to find more expressions and questions you can use in debates. Then report your findings to the class and share them with your classmates.

Comprehensive Input

The following is the lines from the movie *Inherit the Wind*[2] that contain some cross examinations. In the movie, Brady took it upon himself to prosecute a high school biology teacher for including evolution in his curriculum; that was deemed contrary to the Bible and, therefore, contrary to Tennessee law. The trial pitted the great defense attorney Drummond against Brady.

The arrogant Brady, who was at times assisted by co-counsel, took the stand as an expert on the Bible, permitting himself to be cross examined by Drummond. Subject to the court's discretion and stipulation of counsel, an attorney for a party may take the stand to be examined and cross-examined.

Drummond's goal was to show that evolution, or science in general, did not necessarily conflict with biblical doctrine. During the classic cross examination that follows, Drummond managed to shake the otherwise unshakable Brady and his intractably dogmatic claim that the unholy "evil-lution" could never be reconciled with biblical teachings.

Unit 31 Questioning and Team Skills in Debate

Note how Drummond drew his battle line at a single hour of a single day. The simple two-word concession "It's possible" then permitted him to throw his adversary over a temporal mat stretching 10 million years.

Read and imitate the lines afterwards.

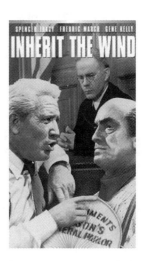

Drummond: [holding up a divided piece of stone] How old do you think this rock is?

Brady: [sarcastically] I am more interested in the Rock of Ages than I am in the age of rocks.

Drummond: Dr. Page of Oberlin College tells me this rock is at least 10 million years old.

Brady: That rock is not more than 6 000 years old.

Drummond: How do you know?

Brady: A fine biblical scholar, Bishop Usher, has determined for us the exact date and hour of the creation. It occurred in the year 4004 B. C.

Drummond: Ah, well, that's ... Bishop Usher's opinion.

Brady: It's not an opinion. It's a literal fact, which the good bishop arrived at through careful computation of the ages of the prophets as set down in the Old Testament. In fact, he determined that the Lord began creation the 23rd of October, 4004 B. C., at 9 a. m.

Drummond: Was that Eastern Standard Time? ... It wasn't Daylight Savings Time, was it? Because the Lord did not make the sun until the fourth day?

Brady: That is correct.

Drummond: That first day, what do you think it was? Twenty-four hours long?

Brady: The Bible says it was a day.

Drummond: Well, but there was no sun out. How do you know how long it was?

Brady: The Bible says it was a day!

Drummond: But was it a normal day? A literal day? A 24-hour day?

Brady: I do not know.

Drummond: What do you think?

Brady: I do not think about things that I do not think about.

Drummond: Do you ever think about things that you do think about? Isn't it possible that it could have been 25 hours? There was no way to measure it, no way to tell. Could it have been 25 hours?

Brady: It's possible.

Drummond: Then you interpret that the first day as recorded in the book of Genesis could have been a day of indeterminate length?

Brady: I mean to state that it is not necessarily a 24-hour day.
Drummond: It could have been 30 hours! Could have been a week! Could have been a month! Could have been a year! Could have been a hundred years ... Could have been 10 million years!

...

Comprehensive Practice

1. Pair Work

Watch the movie and imitate. Act out the movie lines.

2. Group Work

Discuss and analyze how Drummond moved the intractable Brady from a rock-solid position. What single point did he target to win his points in debate?

3. Class Work

1) Work out a proposition that is familiar in campus life. Divide the class into two sides with one for and the other against it. Each side may form smaller groups of three or four and collect evidence and design cross examination questions, especially leading questions for their opponents. Practice arguing for your side.

2) Select three members for your team and organize a debate. Special attention should be put to the cross examination process, and team work should be encouraged.

3) Then the whole class will evaluate the performance of both sides.

Extra Input

Read the following debate excerpt carefully and see how the two argue with each other.

A. T. Still vs. D. D. Palmer

S: You're a thief! You stole my work and labeled it chiropractic.

P: How could I steal that which you never owned?

S: I founded osteopathy in 1874. It is based on the manipulation of the bones of the spine to allow the blood to flow smoothly and without interruption.

P: I founded chiropractic in 1895. It is based on the fundamental of the specific adjustment of the subluxated bones of the spine to free impinged nerves and allow nerve impulses to flow to the body without interruption.

S: I am a physician!

P: I am not a physician!

S: I was a medical doctor long before I founded osteopathy. About 30 years ago, I began to realize the power of nature to cure after a skillful manipulation of conditions to allow pure and healthy blood to flow into the diseased area. With this faith and by this method of reasoning, I began to treat diseases by osteopathic means — and obtained good results.

P: I was not a medical doctor before I founded chiropractic, therefore, my mind was not burdened with medical theories to conflict with the pureness of the chiropractic principle. Chiropractic had no previous theories to wrestle with. It deals with the life force which flows over the nervous system. This power flows from the brain over the nerves as an impulse. This is the primary source of life and health.

S: I hesitated years before proclaiming my new discovery. I finally took my stand on this rock upon which the science of osteopathy was built, where I have stood and fought mighty battles!

P: Perhaps you waited because your education was medical, and it is difficult to get away from those ideas which were thoroughly instilled in your mind. The circulation of blood is simply a channel by means of which food in liquid form is carried to all tissues. Blood is secondary and under the control of the nervous system.

New Hurdles

1. Retelling

Listen to the passage and retell it immediately after you have heard it.

Facing one of the nation's most respected debaters, Republican presidential candidate George W. Bush has proved he can hold his own against more experienced orators.

Although Bush entered the presidential race untested on the national debate stage, he has proved to be a competent, if not spectacular debater. Throughout his short political career, Bush has benefited from low expectations of his debating abilities. He skipped no less than three GOP primary debates, and was reluctant 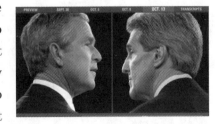 to agree to the Commission on Presidential Debates proposal. Yet, he still gave the impression of a candidate uncomfortable with this unavoidable fact of campaign life.

However, Bush is adept at memorizing and delivering sound bites as well as projecting an air of confidence onstage, and managing to do well in most of his previous debates despite his opponents' best efforts to get him riled. One can be sure that at least a few

Bush supporters will be holding their breath, waiting to see if the Texas governor makes it through this.

In the 1978 congressional race, during a local radio debate against state Sen. Kent Hance, a Democrat, an inexperienced Bush was unable to keep his cool under pressure, becoming visibly angry when asked about his family's ties to the Trilateral Commission and a "one-world government." He was still fuming after the event, cursing the talk-show host and refusing to shake hands.

During a televised 1978 debate, Hance characterized Bush as an Ivy League Washington insider running on his family name. He argued that Washington was corrupt because Yalies like Bush had the run of the place, and noted that in contrast his own "daddy and granddad were farmers. They did not have anything to do with the mess we're in right now, and Bush's father has been in politics his whole life."

2. Talking on a Given Topic

You are required to talk about your opinion about the important influence of one's family or social connections on his performance at school or at work. You can support your opinion by using your own experience or information from reading. You have three minutes to prepare your talk and then give it to your partner.

3. Role Play

The task involves two students, Student A and Student B. Each has a specified role as follows. Although the situation is the same, your roles are different. Learn about the role you want to play. Your preparation time is three minutes. Your conversation is limited to four minutes.

Student A: You are a member of the recruiting committee from a company. Two excellent college graduates, A and B, are applying for a job. A is from a teacher's family and B from a worker's family. You want to employ A but your co-worker wants B. You will try to argue with him/her for your opinion.

Student B: You are another member of the recruiting committee from the same company. You want to employ B instead of A. You will try to argue with your co-worker for your opinion.

Notes

1. Henry Ford (1863—1947): Founder of Ford Motor Company.
2. *Inherit the Wind*: a 1960 Hollywood film based on the play with the same name.

Amusement Park

1. Movie to Enjoy

See the following movie and share your personal view with your classmates.

Silence of the Lamb (1991)

Sweeping all five major Academy Awards ("Oscars" for Best Movie, Director, Actor, Actress, and Screenplay) is quite an accomplishment. Doing it nearly a year after a film was released is a miracle considering the notoriously short attention span of Oscar voters. It is a powerful example of how great a movie can be when superb writers, directors, actors, and others work at the top of their craft.

Young FBI agent Clarice Starling is assigned to help find a missing woman to save her from a psychopathic serial killer who skins his victims. Clarice attempts to gain a better insight into the twisted mind of the killer by talking to another psychopath Hannibal Lecter, who used to be a respected psychiatrist. FBI agent Jack Crawford believes that Lecter, who is also a very powerful and clever mind manipulator, has the answers to their questions to help locate the killer. Clarice must first try and gain Lecter's confidence before he is to give away any information...

Special Highlight

The dialogues between the young, vulnerable Clarice Starling and the chilling, manipulative Hannibal Lecter are very interesting, sometimes horrifying to watch. The dialogues show how speech can be used to exert control and gain the upper hand in a conflict or contest.

Listen to the dialogues carefully and try to observe how the balance of power is shifted in the course of the dialogues.

2. Song to Enjoy

The following is part of the lyrics to the song "There You'll Be" by Faith Hill. Find a recording of the song, listen to it and complete the lyrics.

Does any song affect you in such a way that when you sing them, you think of past experiences and feel strong emotions?

When I think back on these times
and the dreams we left behind

I'll be glad 'cause I was blessed to get
to have you in my life
When I look back on these days
I'll look and see your face
You're right there for me
In my dreams I'll always see you soar above the skies
In my heart there'll always be a place for you
For all my life
I'll keep a part of you with me
And everywhere I am there you'll be
And everywhere I am there you'll be
...

3. Community Learning

Design a debate activity in your class. You may choose a topic on your own and divide the class into three groups — the proposition, the opposition and the "not-decided yet". While the debate is going on, the "not-decided yet" group may choose to join either the proposition or the opposition. See which side can win more people on their side.

Unit 32

Parliamentary Debate

> It is better to debate a question without settling it than to settle a question without debating it.
>
> — Joseph Joubert[1]

Unit Goals

- To learn about British parliamentary debate and American parliamentary debate
- To learn more about the strategies in debating
- To understand the importance of body language in speech delivery

Warm-Up

1. Have you ever seen any debate contest? Which debater has left you the deepest impression? What is most impressive about him/her?
2. What do you think are the qualities of an excellent debater? Do you think you possess some of the qualities?
3. Have you had any experience of debating on certain occasions? Was it a contest or not?
4. If you are to participate in a debate, would you rather be on the side of the proposition or opposition? Why?

Knowledge Input

British Parliamentary Debate

British Parliamentary Debate is very widespread, and has gained major support in the

United Kingdom, Ireland, Europe, Africa, and United States. It has also been adopted as the official style of the World Universities Debating Championship and the European Universities Debating Championship (at which the speakers are given only fifteen minutes' notice of the motion). Speeches are usually between five and seven minutes in duration. The debate consists of four teams of two speakers, called *factions*, with two factions on either side of the case.

Because of the style's origins in British parliamentary procedure, the two sides are called the *Government* and *Opposition*, while the speakers take their titles from those of their parliamentary equivalents (such as the opening Government speaker, called the *Prime Minister*). The speakers are similarly titled:

1. *Opening Government* (first faction)
    1) Prime Minister
    2) Deputy Prime Minister
2. *Opening Opposition* (second faction)
    1) Leader of the Opposition
    2) Deputy Leader of the Opposition
3. *Closing Government* (third faction)
    1) Member for the Government
    2) Government Whip
4. *Closing Opposition* (fourth faction)
    1) Member for the Opposition
    2) Opposition Whip

Speaking alternates between the two sides and the order of the debate is therefore:
1. Prime Minister
2. Opposition Leader
3. Deputy Prime Minister
4. Deputy Opposition Leader
5. Member of the Government
6. Member of the Opposition
7. Government Whip
8. Opposition Whip

As British Parliamentary debates take place between four teams, their roles are split into two categories, those for the Opening Factions, and those for the Closing Factions.

The Opening Factions have four basic roles in a British Parliamentary debate. They

must:
- ✓ Define the motion of the debate.
- ✓ Present their case.
- ✓ Respond to arguments of the opposing first faction.
- ✓ Maintain their relevance during the debate.

While the second two factions must do the following:
- ✓ Introduce a case extension.
- ✓ Establish and maintain their relevance early in the debate.
- ✓ Respond to the arguments of the first factions.
- ✓ Respond to the case extension of the opposing second faction.

Points of Information

Points of Information (POI) are interjections made by members directed at the speech of the member holding the floor, and made from a sitting position. The style demands that all speakers offer POIs to their opposition. POIs are important in British Parliamentary style, as it allows the first two factions to maintain their relevance during the course of the debate, and the last two factions to introduce their arguments early in the debate. The first and last minute of each speech is considered "protected time", during which no points of information may be offered.

American Parliamentary Debate

American Parliamentary Debate is supported by a number of organizations in the United States at the tertiary and secondary levels. The National Parliamentary Debate Association (NPDA) and the American Parliamentary Debate Association (APDA), together with several other organizations, all offer collegiate parliamentary debate.

This style consists of two teams, with the following speakers:
1. *Government*
    1) Prime Minister (PM)
    2) Member of the Government (MG)
2. *Opposition*
    1) Leader of the Opposition (LO)
    2) Member of the Opposition (MO)

In American Parliamentary, the speaking order and timings of each debate is generally:
1. Prime Minister: 7 minutes

2. Leader of the Opposition: 8 minutes
3. Member of the Government: 8 minutes
4. Member of the Opposition: 8 minutes
5. Leader of the Opposition Rebuttal: 4 minutes
6. Prime Minister Rebuttal: 5 minutes

As with any debating style, the individual timings may vary between organizations.

In most variations on the style, Points of Information (POI) may be asked of the speaker during the first four speeches, except during the first and last minute of each speech (this is known as "protected time").

Depending on the variation of the style, the opposing team may interrupt the speaker during a Rebuttal Speech in order to offer one of two kinds of point:

When the speaker is introducing a new argument or grossly mischaracterizing arguments, he or she is raising a Point of Order.

When the speaker makes offensive claims, or personal attacks, he or she is raising a Point of Personal Privilege.

The spirit of Parliamentary Debate is debate that can be taken to the streets. This means that it is easy to understand and educational to all at the same time, regardless of the audience member's expertise of the resolution.

Knowledge Internalization

1. Pair Work

Discuss the following questions after reading the text.

1) What are the four teams in British Parliamentary debate and the two teams in American Parliamentary debate?
2) What is POI? Why is it important in parliamentary debate? What are the two kinds of points?
3) What are the speaking order and timings in British/American Parliamentary debate?
4) In British Parliamentary debate, what are the basic roles of opening/closing factions?
5) What is the spirit of Parliamentary debate?

2. Group Work

Discuss with your group members the procedure of the parliamentary debate. Do you find the design for the debate absolutely fair? Choose a spokesperson to report the results of your discussion to the class.

3. Class Work

Watch the video recordings of parliamentary debates and familiarize yourselves with the format of parliamentary debates.

Lexical Power Build-up

1. Lexical Input

Here are some useful language chunks for parliamentary debate. Practice them until you can say them automatically, but pay special attention to their pronunciation and intonation.

Ladies and gentlemen, we believe...

To discuss the motion, first of all, we should clarify the very important terms in this motion.

Now I'd like to tell you the unique and irreplaceable functions of... in...

Good morning, ladies and gentlemen, our fellow debaters try to persuade our audience that..., which is not the case from our point of view.

We believe that... and the reasons are as follows.

Let's have a clear knowledge about what the crucial factors really are concerning the...

Thank you for the important issues raised by our dear friends from the affirmative side.

But, as you mentioned in the clarification of definitions, I have to say that by defining... as..., you are committing two fundamental mistakes.

We have never denied the significance of... but that's not the aim for today's discussion.

It's ridiculous for our friends from the other side to ask us whether we are debating about..., but we are discussing.... That is a logical problem.

Here, I'd like to use an easy example to explain this point because this is important.

This is visibly illustrated by the story of...

So to sum up, firstly,...; secondly,...; and thirdly,... We firmly believe that...

2. Solo Work

Practice the useful expressions in the right intonation until you can say them properly and forcefully.

3. Solo Work

Construct complete sentences with the chunks given above and rehearse your sentences.

4. Pair Work

Consider the motion "Governments should not rescue failing private industry".

One of you is the Prime Minister, and the other is the leader of the opposition. The PM is supposed to define a motion and develop the case briefly, using the chunks provided above. The leader of the opposition is to respond and extend.

Comprehensive Input

The following is a speech made by the Prime Minister based on the topic "Urbanization helps improve the quality of living".

Prime Minister: Ladies and gentlemen, we firmly believe that urbanization does help improve quality of living. According to the New Oxford Dictionary of English, urbanization is a process of taking or becoming urban in character. So urbanization goes beyond the physical expansion of urban and the growth of the urban population. Actually, instead, the essence of urbanization is a process to take in urban characteristics, which mainly include three aspects: the first one is high productivity. We know that concentration of resources, investment and science and technology, which takes place in urbanization, provides better working conditions and better research conditions for people to develop their production. On the other hand, the concentration of labor and occupational specialization swiftly enhances efficiency. Consequently, urban areas have higher productivity, and because of this, people can produce more and more material wealth and people can enjoy more and more material comforts. Cities like Birmingham and Liverpool in Britain, and Silicon Valley in the US, and Beijing and Shanghai in China, are all good examples.

The second aspect is systematic planning and regulation. In urban areas, as people live together, it is very convenient for them to communicate with each other. So the cost of planning and regulation is low and the efficiency is high. From the layout of the whole district of urban areas to the enforcement of the legal system, from the arrangement of roads to the regulation of the market, every corner of an urban area shows its beauty of systematic planning and regulation. So, this will enhance the efficiency of regulation and will increase the productivity and give people a sense of security.

The third aspect is cultural prosperity and diversity. Urban areas shorten the distance between people, so there is necessity and possibility for people to exchange ideas. This is indispensable for the creative mind. That is why urban areas are the center and cradle of science, culture and fashion. Robber Epock, known as "the Father of American Urbanologist", declares not only that urban areas are the containers of culture but also the cradle of culture, the carrier of culture, and the media of culture communication.

As for quality of living, it is easier, better for us to discuss it on two levels: material satisfaction and spiritual satisfaction. It is not hard to see that these three aspects can improve the quality of life both in terms of material satisfaction and spiritual satisfaction. However, we never say urbanization is a perfect process. Yet problems in the process of urbanization have been solved and more can be solved through further urbanization. For example, the pollution situation has become much better in cities like London and Vienna; and the advantages of urbanization far outweigh its disadvantages. Urban areas, created by human beings themselves, serve the purpose of providing better quality of life from the first day of its growth. To believe in the bright future of urbanization is to believe in the great ability of human beings to improve our quality of life. This belief is finally and exactly what we want to convey to you. Thank you very much.

Comprehensive Practice

1. Pair Work

Analyze the logical pattern of the sample speech and find out how the speaker builds up his/her point.

2. Group Work

Work as a group to create a counter-argument that can be used by the Leader of Opposition. Pay special attention to:

1) the definition of the motion;
2) the presentation of your case;
3) proper and relevant response to arguments made by the PM.

3. Class Work

Complete the following activity.
1) Divide the whole class into 4 groups.
2) Within each group, there are two teams representing the government and the opposition respectively.
3) Each group is supposed to do research work before deciding on one of the following motions:
   - A nation's best athletes have a duty to represent their country in the Olympic Games.

- The Olympic Games promote unhealthy nationalism.
- The interval between Olympic Games should be shortened.

4) Debate in the American Parliamentary format within the group.
5) Select one group to present their debate in the class. The rest of the class analyze and comment on their debate.

4. Solo Work

Gestures

Gestures usually mean movements of hands and arms, but a small movement of any part of the body could as well be considered a gesture. A gesture is always purposeful. They add meaning and effectiveness to the speaker's language.

Gestures in debate should be as natural and appropriate as they are in conventional speech. The hands act spontaneously as the words are spoken.

There are two types of gestures: emphatic and demonstrative. In a sense, all gestures are demonstrative and all are emphatic, but because they are usually more one than the other, it is useful to think of them separately.

Now stand in front of the mirror and read some sentences from the sample speech or from the speech you have created. Practice using gestures while trying to make a point.

5. Pair Work

Examine the action of your instructors as well as your classmates. Prepare as long a list as possible of actions which are effective and actions which are distracting. Discuss whether or not there is any relationship between good vocal action and good physical action.

6. Solo Work

Practice your speech in front of a full-length mirror. Keep yourself erect and practice some strong action — positive, clear-cut movement and definite arm and hand gestures. Intentionally overdo it to help free your body.

7. Group Work

The class is divided into groups of four. Within each group, there are two teams representing the government and the opposition respectively. Decide on one of the following motions; do the research and debate in the American parliamentary format:

- The use of animals for sport should be abolished;
- China should prohibit the production of animals for their fur;

- China should create standards for the ethical treatment of animals.

Extra Input

Study the speeches made by both Government and Opposition based on the motion: This House believes that animals belong in their natural habitat.

Learn how the speakers make their assertions with force and relevance. Decide which side has done a better job, the Government or the Opposition and state your reasons.

Government	Opposition
Animals belong in their natural habitat in the wild. It is a breach of their natural rights to take them by force into captivity for our own purposes.	Animals do not have rights. In any case, zoos, as we will see below, exist to protect endangered species and to help us understand and protect our animal cousins more successfully. One of the reasons animals are taken into captivity in zoos is because they are under threat if they stay in their natural habitat.
Whatever the good intentions of zoo-keepers, animals in zoos suffer. They are inevitably confined in unnaturally small spaces, and are kept from the public by cages and bars. They suffer psychological distress, often displayed by abnormal or self-destructive behavior. Aquatic animals do not have enough water, birds are prevented from flying away by having their wings clipped and being kept in aviaries.	There have been many bad zoos and cruel zookeepers in the past. It is imperative that these are reformed and weeded out. Good zoos in which animals are well fed and well looked after in spacious surroundings are becoming the norm and should be encouraged. Zoos can exist without cruelty to animals, however, and so the fact that there are animal welfare problems with some zoos does not mean that all zoos should be shut down.
Adults and children visiting zoos will be given the subliminal message that it is OK to use animals for our own ends. However, it impinges on their freedom or quality of life; thus zoos generally encourage poor treatment of animals. People do not go to zoos for educational reasons, they simply go to be entertained and diverted by weird and wonderful creatures seen as objects of beauty or entertainment. As a form of education the zoo is deficient: the only way to understand an animal properly is to see it in its natural environment. The zoo gives a totally artificial and misleading view of the animal by isolating it from its ecosystem.	Zoos nowadays are not marketed as places of entertainment — they are places of education. Most modern zoos have their main emphasis on conservation and education — the reason that so many schools take children to zoos is to teach them about nature, the environment, endangered species, and conservation. Far from encouraging bad treatment of animals, zoos provide a direct experience of other species that will increase ecological awareness.

Government	Opposition
There are two problems with the claim that zoos are beneficial because they help to conserve endangered species. First, they do not have a very high success rate — many species are going extinct each week despite the good intentions of some zoos. This is partly because a very small captive community of a species is more prone to inter-breeding and birth defects. Secondly, captive breeding to try to stave off extinction need not take place in the context of a zoo, where the public come to look at captive animals and (often) see them perform tricks. Captive breeding programs should be undertaken in large nature reserves, not within the confines of a zoo.	One of the main functions of zoos is to breed endangered animals in captivity. If natural or human factors have made a species' own habitat a threatening environment, then human intervention can preserve that species where it would certainly go extinct if there were no intervention. There are certainly problems with trying to conserve endangered species in this way, but it is right that we should at least try to conserve them. And as long as animals are treated well in zoos there is no reason why conservation, education, and cruelty-free entertainment should not all be combined in a zoo. There is also, of course, a valid role for breeding in different environments such as large nature reserves.
As above, research into animals (when it respects their rights and is not cruel or harmful) may be valuable, but it does not need to happen in the context of confinement and human entertainment. Also, the only way really to understand other species is to study them in their natural habitat and see how they interact socially and with other species of flora and fauna.	As above we should take a "both-and" approach rather than an "either-or" approach. Animals can and should be studied in the wild but they can be studied more closely, more rigorously, and over a more sustained period of time in captivity. Both sorts of study are valuable and, as in point 4, there is no reason why this should not be done in the context of a cruelty-free zoo as well as in other contexts.

New Hurdles

1. Retelling

Listen to the passage and retell it immediately after you have heard it.

It has been a year and a half since I began to learn about parliamentary debate and participate in training and practices. It gets me out of several English learning traps and gets me into a habit of doubting and thinking.

Debating reinforces a concept that language is for communication and that language is a carrier of culture. By debating in English, we are not showing off our elegant British accent or fluent American English. Neither are we competing for who can use more paralleled structures or other figures of speech. Instead, we are exchanging our ideas using logic and reasoning typical in the culture revealed by the language — English. In this sense, we may say that parliamentary debate is a true form of English debating while the form of free debate is only Chinese pattern of thinking packed in an English box.

And thanks to parliamentary debate, I have gotten out of several English-learning traps, naming, overemphasizing pronunciation and expression. Of course it does no harm if one speaks with an authentic British accent and can use numerous quotations and beautiful expressions. But when it comes to the extent that it affects your flow of expressing ideas, you have to think twice to decide which element gets priority. The answer is a natural flow of ideas comes first.

By saying that we should first of all convey the message, I do not mean that we should not pay attention to wording. The proper choice of words matters a lot in driving home your message as precisely as possible. Using an inappropriate word may even distort your intention and weaken your arguments. The ultimate goal is to make our ideas clear using simple and appropriate language.

Having said all these about language, I'd like to share with you what I've gained in parliamentary debate in terms of new perspectives to observe the world.

More often than not, I hear people say that girls only care about trivial things happening around themselves and have a very shallow understanding of events of importance. And there are also similar comments on students of liberal arts, saying that their ideas are "soft and silly". Unfortunately I am both a girl and a student of liberal arts. I must admit at least I only focused on my own business and thought little about the society before I learned about parliamentary debate. It is no exaggeration that debate has changed my pattern of thinking, my way of treating life and the world around me. I have started to listen to different voices expressing different attitudes towards current affairs, both home and abroad. I have learned to put aside my preoccupation or prejudice against certain groups and issues and hold a tolerant mind to take in various opinions. I have begun to think on my own feet instead of blindly follow the so-called authorities. Everything is worth thinking about and nothing is doubt-proof.

2. Talking on a Given Topic

You are required to talk about your experience participating in a debate or watching a debate. Tell what the debate was about and how the debate affected you. You have three minutes to prepare your talk and then talk to your partner.

3. Role Play

The task involves two students, Student A and Student B. Each has a specified role as follows. Although the situation is the same, your roles are different. Learn about the role you want to play. Your preparation time is three minutes. Your conversation is limited to four minutes.

Student A: Today, lots of famous people in China, such as athletes, are admitted to famous universities without taking the college entrance exam. You and your partner are discussing the issue. You think these people deserve a chance since they have contributed a lot to the country. Your partner does not agree. Try to convince him/her. Remember you should start the conversation.

Student B: Today, lots of famous people in China, such as athletes, are admitted to famous universities without taking the college entrance exam. You and your partner are discussing the issue. You do not think these people should be given this chance since it is unfair to the other people who work so hard to pass the exam. Your partner does not agree. Try to convince him/her. Remember your partner should start the conversation.

Notes

1. Joseph Joubert (1754 — 1824): French moralist and essayist.

Amusement Park

1. Movie to Enjoy

See the following movie and share your personal view with your classmates.

Click (2006)

Michael Newman seems to have a perfect life — a beautiful wife, two small children, and a job with great potential. But as his jerky boss passes Michael up for promotion after promotion, Michael becomes fed up, and wishes he could find a way to skip through the hard parts in life. He gets exactly that — and much, much more — when he stumbles upon the Beyond section of a Bed, Bath, and Beyond in search of a universal remote. But as it turns out, the remote controls the entire universe! ...

Special Highlight

In the movie, Michael Newman has a remote which can control the universe, anticipating and interpreting his wishes. Are you willing to fast-forward yourself several years and skip your current disappointments? Why or why not?

2. Song to Enjoy

The following is part of the lyrics to the song "Flying without Wings" by Westlife. Find a recording of the song, listen to it and complete the lyrics.

How can we fly without wings? What is that something everyone is looking for? Are you expecting it, too?

>Everybody's looking for that something
>One thing that makes it all complete
>You'll find it in the strangest places
>Places you never knew it could be
>
>Some find it in the face of their children
>Some find it in their lovers' eyes
>Who can deny the joy it brings
>When you've found that special thing
>You're flying without wings
>
>Some find it sharing every morning
>Some in their solitary lives
>You'll find it in the words of others
>A simple line can make you laugh or cry
>...

3. Community Learning

Form groups of 5 to 7 students for a Panel Discussion. Follow the following directions.

Roles: panel leader
school principal
teacher
students
parents

Topic: Should China abolish English as a compulsory subject in postgraduate entrance examinations?

Procedure:

1) Each student chooses a role.
2) The panel leader starts the discussion by introducing the panel members and the

topic. It is the responsibility of the panel leader to make sure that each member has a say and that the discussion goes smoothly. The following questions might be used to elicit speech:

- ✓ Would you please say something, Mr./Ms. ...?
- ✓ What do you have to say about this, Mr./Ms. ...?
- ✓ Perhaps you could tell us how students normally look at this issue?

3) Group members speak impromptu on the topic or answer the questions asked.
4) Select one or two groups to conduct the panel discussion before the class. The audience is encouraged to raise questions for the panel members.

参 考 文 献

[1] ESCHHOLZ P and ALFRED R. Language Awareness. Bedford:Boston,2000.
[2] HAMILTON C. Essentials of Public Speaking. Peking University Press:Beijing,2003.
[3] LUCAS S E. The Art of Public Speaking. Foreign Language Teaching and Research Press:Beijing,2007.
[4] SCHNEIDER K and MCCOLLUM S. It's Academic. Maxwell Macmillan:Ontario,1991.
[5] SMALLEY L R and MARY K R. Refining Composition Skills. Heinle & Heinle:Boston,2001.
[6] STEVEN B R and SCOTT M D. Between One and Many. McGraw-Hill companies, Inc.:Boston,2003.
[7] 胡曙中. 英汉修辞跨文化研究[M]. 青岛:青岛出版社,2008.
[8] 贾国栋. 2001—2007美国总统广播讲话精选[M]. 北京:外语教学与研究出版社,2008.
[9] 刘亚猛. 西方修辞学史[M]. 北京:外语教学与研究出版社,2008.
[10] 马德高. 英语演讲高手[M]. 济南:山东科学技术出版社,2008.
[11] 《外研之声》编辑部. "外研社杯"全国英语辩论赛[M]. 北京:外语教学与研究出版社,2004.
[12] 西塞罗. 西塞罗全集·修辞学卷[M]. 王晓朝,译. 北京:人民出版社,2007.
[13] 许力生. 跨语言研究的跨文化视野[M]. 上海:上海外语教育出版社,2006.
[14] 亚里士多德. 修辞学[M]. 上海:上海人民出版社,2006.
[15] http://www.americanrhetoric.com
[16] http://www.best-speech-topics.com
[17] http://www.en.wikisource.org/wiki
[18] http://www.grammar.about.com/od/developingparagraphs/a/samdescpars.htm
[19] http://www.great-quotes.com
[20] http://www.inspire21.com/site/stories/
[21] https://www.movies.msn.com/search/movies/
[22] http://www.thinkexist.com
[23] http://www.uefap.com/speaking/function/describe.htm